Turning God's Face

TURNING GOD'S FACE

Steve Dragert

WestBow
PRESS
A DIVISION OF THOMAS NELSON

WestBow Press books may be ordered through booksellers or by contacting:

WestBow Press
A Division of Thomas Nelson
1663 Liberty Drive
Bloomington, IN 47403
www.westbowpress.com
1-(866) 928-1240

ISBN: 978-1-4497-4911-8 (sc)

Library of Congress Control Number: 2012907936

Printed in the United States of America

WestBow Press rev. date: 07/05/2012

ACKNOWLEDGEMENTS

My son David D.

For giving me the first chapter

My daughter Lori G.

For giving me the encouragement

My cousin Patt B.

For making the book correct

My friend Johnny J.

For giving me the last chapter

My friend Bob B.

For giving me a push in the right direction

My friend Denise H.

For giving me support

My wife Patt

For being all things to me

The Holy Spirit

For without whom the book could never have been

TABLE OF CONTENTS

FOREWORD

As Father Thomas Kennedy hurried from the rectory to the church for Saturday confessions, he was shocked to discover many dead sparrows along the pathway. He hurriedly made arrangements to have them removed before the children arrived.

The first penitent was a young boy who confessed to trying to kill his sister's cat. Although he did not succeed, he showed no remorse, in fact, bragged about his evil doings. Father Tom was totally alarmed with the boy's attitude.

While attending a school board meeting where she spoke against their continuing efforts to remove any reference to God or spirituality from the schools, DeeDee was struck down by some invisible force, breaking her legs.

Larry explained he had seen things in the wild which defied logical explanation and now was plagued with recurring dreams which also made no sense. Dreams... which were creating extreme anxiousness.

Perhaps because of the recent confessions he heard, Father Tom began having bad dreams as well; not frightening, but an emptiness, the absence of light. Then he discovered his friend and neighboring priest,

Father Terry Fenwick, was experiencing the same dream-filled sleepless nights.

They decided to hold a meeting and invite those who had come to them seeking advice with similar complaints. All expressed feelings of pain, confusion, anxiety, fear, sorrow and were becoming ill with lack of sleep.

With nothing resolved at the gathering, it was brought to the attention of the Bishop and then, with his support, presented to James Cardinal Roan.

Bishop Blom told the Cardinal, "Society has diligently tried to remove GOD, Christian or not, from our public lives." When Cardinal Roan was convinced that it was GOD, not leaving us, but, with a heavy heart, turning away from His people, he organized a DAY OF PRAYER.

It was to be a public showing of unity and solidarity of all faiths, lasting for one week. With hope and humility people all over the country sent prayers of petition with renewed passion and commitment to GOD. And so it happened that The faithful did indeed turn GOD's face, once again toward his believers.

Love, Patt Bohaty

CHAPTER ONE

TOMMY K.

Tommy Kennedy was fourteen years old when the thought first came to him. It was really more of a thought given to him by Sister Mary Ann, the art teacher at St. Agnes high school. "Have you ever thought about becoming a priest?" She posed. "Not really. Why?" Tommy asked. "You have a very deep faith and I know that you are good with people. Besides, the church needs more priests." she answered. Tommy responded, "I don't have real good grades, and I know you have to learn Latin. I even flunked Spanish and that's the easiest language to learn." "Listen Tommy, if God wants you, He'll give you the ability to learn anything you need. Besides, not all the saints were great learners. Some had the 'calling' but not the ability. God took care of that for them and He will take care of that for you. I think you should talk to Father Ryan about going into the seminary." Tommy was hesitant, "Let me think about it, Sister." She responded, "Don't just think about it Tommy, pray about it. The Holy Ghost will answer you and lead you in the right direction. I'll pray too."

Nobody else had ever brought up the subject of being a priest to Tommy, so this was a new experience for him and he started watching the two priests in his parish more closely. He did pray about it and he watched carefully. Monsignor Rhone was an old German who ran the parish with an iron fist. The kids called him "the Mons" but not to his face. Most of the kids in the grade school, as well as the high school, were intimidated by his gruff personality. The adults, on the other hand, loved him. He had a great sense of humor that he showed only to the adults. None of the children saw anything but a strong religious leader whom you didn't disrespect. Father Ryan Davies was exactly the opposite. He loved the kids and they loved him. Most of his "off" time was spent in the grade school's gym playing basketball. He was never alone. There was always one or two of the parish kids hanging around to shoot hoops with him. He related to the adults, but not like he felt with kids hanging around him. Fr. Ryan seemed to have a stronger faith than The Mons, at least, that is how the children felt. The Mons was hard and a disciplinarian, where Fr. Ryan was more of a confessor and friend. Tommy watched them both carefully. He watched at school, at Mass when he was an altar boy, or when they thought they were alone saying their daily office. Tommy watched so he could make a better, more informed decision about what Sr. Mary Ann had put in his head.

The question remained with him all through high school and when Patricia England caught his eye in the junior year, he put the question to its hardest test. Pat and he started going steady six months later. He asked her if she wanted to be exclusive, at the prom under the blue lights of the prom's theme. She was delighted to accept his ring, as a sign of their commitment to date only each other.

"The Mons" called that activity "an occasion of sin" and highly recommended against the practice. But "puppy love" would not be ignored. Their occasion of sin never became an actual sin, more Pat's decision than Tommy's though.

When graduation time came to end their high school experience, Pat's family moved out of state and Tommy again had deep thoughts about his future. The question of becoming a priest loomed in his heart and mind. His last year in high school was a delight to his parents and a surprise to his teachers. Tommy had made the honor role for the first time in his years of education, grade school or high school. Tommy was surprised as well and wondered if the good grades were a sign from on high. In his heart he knew the answer, but his head kept making excuses.

Sr. Mary Ann had suggested that he talk to Fr. Ryan and Tommy kept putting off the conversation, even though she had made that suggestion at least a hundred times in the last two years. Tommy went up to the gym in the late afternoon one Saturday. Fr. Ryan was shooting baskets with seven of the older grade school kids. He went in and sat in one of the bleacher seats. Watching the priest and kids enjoying their game, Tommy started forming his questions to the priest. It seemed like seven hours but was only one half hour before Ryan saw him sitting there in deep thought. Ryan tossed the ball to one of the kids, grabbed a towel, wiped his face and wrapped it around his neck as he walked over to Tommy. The priest sat down next to the high school graduate. "You're Tommy Kennedy, aren't you?" "Yes Father." "Do you need to see me or were you just here to watch those boys shoot hoops better than me?" Tommy was slow to answer even though he had been working on his questions for a half hour. "Father, do you think I'd be a good priest?" Ryan asked: "Do you think you would be a good priest, Tommy?" "I don't know Father, I think so, but I don't really know." Ryan answered, "Tommy, have you talked to your family about this?"

Tommy's parents had four children. Tommy was the oldest. His Father, Willard Louis Kennedy (nicknamed Jess because of a famous boxer named Jess Willard, long since forgotten) insisted that his first born son would carry his name and told his fiancée, Barbara, that fact before anything else was to be decided, if they were to marry.

Barbara didn't like the name Willard. It wasn't a Christian name like William, but she agreed at the time, yet planned a future discussion about the name of their first born. In a short six months they walked down the aisle at St. Agnes church. One year later Tommy was born and Barbara had the difficult task now upon her, to change her husband's mind about naming their son. She talked gently to Willard about his name and after much discussion (Willard wasn't going to argue with a new mother) Tommy was named Thomas Joseph. After Tommy was born his brother Robert, called Robbie, was born deaf, but with the biggest blue eyes anyone had ever seen. Then the girls were born. There were two years between each of the four children in the Kennedy family. Robbie and Susan the next oldest had the same birthday, May 14th, only two years apart.

Laura was the youngest and was treated by the older boys as their own personal doll, while they were young. As the years rolled by the doll thing became more of a pest thing. They picked on Laura who always wanted to be with her big brothers, though nobody knew why, especially when they picked on her so. "Be nice to your sister, soon she will be big enough to not want to be around you two anymore." Their mother, Barbara, would scold them. It was a happy family with only the natural and expected quarrelling of siblings that was no more serious than it was mean. The two girls adored their older brothers and the boys always protected the girls from known, as well as perceived dangers. Barbara had a garden in the back yard that was her love and all the family had a part of growing the garden.

The boys would help their father till the ground in preparation for the spring planting. The girls would help Mom plant the seedlings and the whole family would do with the weeding. It was a summer long proposition which drew the family into a strong group with one objective in sight.

It was in the garden that Tommy first approached the possibility of becoming a priest with his mother. His father was not Catholic so approaching him with the idea was not Tommy's first choice. Jess would not have been dead set against the idea but he wouldn't have the whole picture of the commitment necessary to do the priestly duties. This is what Tommy thought at the beginning. He was wrong.

After talking to Tommy, Barbara addressed the situation with her husband. His reaction even surprised her. Jess told her that he thought Tommy should be a priest and had thought so for some time. He told her: "Tommy would come home from school, directly to me with a new discovery about being a Catholic. I could see the joy and happiness just a bouncing off his face. I would challenge him to prove whatever it was that he discovered and that sent him to the Bible every time.

I think he learned more from those challenges than he ever did in school from the nuns. I was sure he was going to follow that path all along. I'm surprised you didn't!"

Now with his parents on board, it was an easier path to the seminary. Fr. Ryan introduced him to Father Paul Lowery. Paul, the vocation director for the diocese, was responsible for interviewing each candidate for the seminary. The interview was set up for after school. Fr. Paul met him in one of the smaller classrooms and they would talk there for however long it might take. Tommy was more nervous than he had expected, as he walked into the classroom and shook hands with Fr. Paul. Fr. Paul was an extremely friendly man, round in appearance with a bald head and a smile that never left his face. He was easy to talk to, the very reason he was selected by the bishop to fill this important position.

"Tell me young Tom, why are we here today?" "Fr. Ryan told me I had to talk to you if I wanted to get into the seminary." Paul laughed loudly, "Well that's the God's truth. You have to go through me. That's for sure. But Tom, I really want to know why you feel the need of becoming a priest?" Tom responded, "I don't know. I just know that it is something I have to do." "Let's talk about that Tom. You really don't know why, but you really want to do this thing. Explain that a little more if you can, Tom." Tom thought for what seemed a long time, "I know deep inside that being a priest is what God wants me to do. I know that it would call for a lot of study to get there, but I think God showed me that I can do that too. After the seminary I am sure that the life of a priest, serving God and His people, is just where I want to be." The conversation went on for about an hour with Paul laughing encouragement to the young man and Tom trying desperately to explain his heart's desires to the friendly priest. "Well, young Tom, I think you will be a great asset to the seminary.

Let me explain something important to you about your future education. The seminary is a college first and a 'priest maker' second. The diocese will pay for your education, but if you drop out, you owe the diocese for that education.

Is that understood?" Tommy told him that he understood and Paul explained that there would be paperwork forthcoming that would bind him to that agreement. Tom was heading to the seminary for his freshman year in college.

Going off to college, located away from home, was the same for every first year student all across the nation. Tom's experience was no different. Jess and Barbara, accompanied by all their kids, drove to the small town in Iowa where Tommy would spend the next four years of his life.

His roommate was a tall, good looking redhead who had the strange name of Tobias Wrinkle. Toby and Tom would become very close friends within the next four years, but on this first day they were strangers whose family members numbered fifteen in total. The small dormitory room, they shared, would not accommodate all the family members, so some were in the hallway, waiting their turn to look at the room's interior. The two families decided to go to lunch together at a nearby fast food restaurant. Over the hamburgers, there was much laughter and getting to know each other. Later that day, when all had gone home Tom and Toby lay in their beds recollecting all that was fun about that day. Many more days and nights were in their future where exactly the same thing would occur. There would be conversations about, faith, sex, grades, music, sports, theology and family. This night there was only the conversation meant to enable the two young men to better know each other. It was the beginning.

CHAPTER TWO

FATHER TOM KENNEDY

Tom Kennedy had been a priest for 23 years and his mother was looking forward to celebrating the 25th anniversary of his ordination in two years. Tom, too, was looking to the future and that celebration. He remembered the day he laid prone at the foot of the altar in the cathedral, and listened to the Bishop as he celebrated the Mass and ordained all five of his brothers in Christ. Tom loved all seven of the sacraments but he lived Holy Orders on a daily basis and never regretted his choice to follow his "Calling" as his mother named it. He loved the sacrament of confession as much as the other six, but there was always a part of that celebration of Christ's life here on earth that he didn't look forward to. It was the constant belief of the parishioners who entered the confessional, that they had committed the worst sin ever in the history of the world. Tom felt the close feeling of God's love when he heard the confessions. He felt the special feeling of a priest understanding the sorrow of sinners needing forgiveness and understanding that through this act, their sins were forgiven. But they sometimes told the same sin over and over, not content to hear him say "your sins are forgiven.", not fully believing the truth of the sacrament. Then there were the confessions of the nuns who taught at the school. Tom told his priest friends and some of his close friends who were not clergy that hearing the confession of a nun was like being beaten to death with a feather.

He left the rectory, a simple house on the same campus as the school and the church, and was walking to the church that Saturday afternoon for the purpose of hearing confessions that would start at 2:00pm just like any other Saturday afternoon. The stone walkway that had been put down by some parishioners long before Tom was assigned to St. Joseph, but after the rectory and the church had been built. It was his path to the church. He wore a gray pullover sweat shirt and his uniform black pants with white tennis shoes. He didn't need to show the priestly appearance while behind the screen that separated the two sides of the confessional. He could hear when a confessor would enter. To assist the priests, there was an electric contact on the kneeler, and when someone would kneel the contact would light the small red bulb in his chamber. There were two bulbs, one for the right and one for the left. As Tom walked to the church he noticed a small clump of tan, brown, black and white on one of the stones in his path. When he got close enough he realized it was a dead sparrow.

He picked it up and was going to throw it into the bushes located on the side of the church when he thought of the passage in the bible from Matthew that reminds us that "Our Father knows when a sparrow falls and that we are even more Important in His eyes."

It was a comforting thought and he put it in the back of his mind, ready to use for a sermon some Sunday soon. Tom was lost in that thought as he walked towards the church and it surprised him to see yet another fallen sparrow near the maple tree to his right. He looked around the grounds to his left and right, then in the direction of the church. There were maybe 20 dead sparrows in the yard. The one in his hand suddenly became repugnant to him and he let it fall from his palm. What had caused the death of these birds? Why had they fallen here in the yard between the rectory and the church? He sped up his walk. He intended to notify the maintenance man, Bill Thomas, to clean up the grounds before some of the children, who were sent to the church every Saturday at 2:00pm, by their parents, would find them there. He pulled the cell phone from his pocket and called the rectory number. Gladys answered and he explained to the housekeeper what he saw on the way to the church. She said that she would make sure that Bill would get the problem taken care of post haste. It didn't set right with Tom as he entered the confessional. This was not a pleasant sight. The question of what had happened may never get answered, though he was going to do his best to find out.

The first three confessors told nothing unusual in their need for forgiveness and Tom gave them absolution. The first ten parishioners who entered the small chambers were adults. Tom was thankful that the children hadn't had the opportunity to come upon the death he had found on the walk. He hoped and prayed that was the case anyway. The next person to enter the confessional was a young boy maybe about 10 years old. He started his confession, "Bless me Father, for I have sinned. My last confession was a week ago. Since then I lied twice to my teacher, I took some gum from my brother and I tried to kill my sister's cat." Tom smiled to himself and asked, without letting the boy hear his smile, "You tried to kill your sister's cat?" "Yes Father, I tried but didn't get it done." The response brought a bigger smile to Tom's face. He was sure that the boy was exaggerating what he had done to the cat. He just couldn't believe a young boy who comes to confession on a regular basis would really do the deed. He probably thought it was more horrendous a situation than it really was. "Tell me what you did, son." asked Tom. "I tied it to the tree outside, in the back yard. It squealed and spit, but I had the rope tight around its neck real good, so when it started jumping around I just wound the rope around the tree real tight. Then I poured gas on it. I was going to light it up with some matches, but my sister came runnin' out of the house and saved it. I guess that was a sin, but at the time I did it, I didn't care none."

Tom stopped smiling. The boy had an attitude about him that scared the priest. It was more than a childish prank and Tom could sense something deeply disturbing about what the boy had just told him. Tom was, for the first time in all the years of hearing confessions, at a loss. He had heard more serious sins, the sins that the church described as mortal sins. A mortal sin was a willful action that caused the sinner to break any relationship with God. It is defined as turning away from the face of God. Tom knew that the confession he had just heard was even more chilling than the mortal sins he had heard and in Christ's name forgiven.

The confession was heard and it was his obligation, if he believed the boy was sorrowful for his sin, to give him a penance and forgive him the sins. Tom hesitated. He didn't hear any contrition in the boy's story of the cat incident. He needed to ask more questions yet he didn't want to hear any thing more from this kid. Tom's head and heart were in direct conflict with his spiritual being. He was a Catholic priest who was acting on Christ's part to hear and forgive the sins of God's children. He had done his part for 23 years as required by Christ, the church, and his own spirituality. Tom fought his very being and asked the boy, "Are you sorry that you sinned against one of God's creatures and hurt your sister's feelings?" It was a simple question and a start on the roadway to absolution for the boy, yet when given, his answer again brought a cold chill to Tom's whole body. The boy simply responded. "No!' Tom said, "I'm sorry. I can not give you absolution until you are truly sorry for your sins. You need to pray about what you have done and ask Jesus to help you feel sorry that you have hurt someone and sorry that you have tried to hurt an innocent creature of God. You must feel inside that you won't do it again and that you are sorry for what you have already done. You need to pray very hard about those things I've just told you and then come back here as soon as you are sorry." The boy told Tom, "I don't really care. I ain't never commin' back here. I just came here 'cause my Mom told me to. You can go to hell! You can all go to hell! I don't care!"

The light on that side of the confessional went off as the boy left the chamber. Tom wanted to look out and see who it was but he sat there in shock. The shock was not because of hearing a sinner's confess but because of how the boy had told his story. There was a hollow, empty hole from which words of venom came erupting to the surface, none of which Tom had ever experienced before. The red bulb on the other side had been lit during the boy's time in the chamber. Now the bulb, on the boy's side again was turned on by someone kneeling down. Tom wanted to run. For the first time in his life as a priest, he wanted to run from the sacrament of confession and never come back.

He needed to open the small sliding wooden door and reveal the dark screen that kept the person on the other side of the confessional anonymous. The screen did its job as the chambers, all three, were dark except for the red bulb in the center chamber, and those lights didn't provide any illumination within. He sat there too long a period of time. The individual on Tom's right started a series of polite coughs intended to alert the priest that someone was ready to confess. Finally Tom opened the little door and heard confessions of those who had contrition and whose sins he could absolve in Christ's name and authority.

It was 4:00pm and an hour before the Sabbath Mass when Tom heard the last confession. He walked the stone path back to the rectory not being able to put the day's happenings out of his mind nor in any perspective. Something was really wrong and he needed to get to a place where he could make some sense of it. He needed to pray.

CHAPTER THREE

THE SCHOOL BOARD MEETING

Dorothy was called Dee Dee by everyone who knew her. She had met and fallen in love with a man named Thomas Derrick. From the time they were married and she had the initials of D.D. Tom called her Dee Dee and it stuck. She was driving to the school board meeting where she would meet the other members of the Nazarene church whom she had finally convinced to accompany her to this meeting. The last three Wednesday evening services she had talked Pastor Dave into allowing her to lead the discussion. Her topic was "Taking God out of Schools". She had been fired up when she first approached Pastor Dave about the subject. She had seen the topic discussed on an Oprah show and found herself talking to the TV as so many people do when the screen presents a subject that stimulates those deep feelings associated with a topic. She was resolved to do something about the board's decision to remove any reference to God from their public schools. There were 15 fellow members of the church equally interested in this mission to address the board at this meeting. The group from the church consisted of parents, grandparents, an uncle and two students who were from the very school where the meeting was going to take place this evening.

Dee Dee was excited and nervous at the same time. She was confident that she was right in her quest and positive she would have the support for her position within the church group that agreed to accompany her. Yet she had no experience in talking to a large group and heard it said that the fear of public speaking was the most common of people's fears. Dee Dee had that fear this night. She went over the speech she had prepared, in her mind, as she drove to the school named East Mission Road High School. It was a familiar drive. She had graduated from the high school 15 years earlier. It had changed in those years only in philosophy not in appearance. The red brick facade was a comfortable sight and brought a nice warm feeling of contentment to those who had attended and graduated from there. The liberal tones of those who now dictated the way the high school presents itself to the community changed those nice warm feeling's of contentment for Dee Dee. At first she was saddened by the changes. When the school board and the school superintendent announced to the public that they were going to remove certain books from the library that could be associated with or encouraging Christianity, she became upset. She followed with more than a little interest, the newspaper accounts of the board and the superintendent's continuing efforts to get God removed from her school.

She saw it in the paper on that Monday morning just four weeks ago. They were at it again. The article was entitled: **No Prayer in Mission Road High School Any More**. They now were preventing prayer in any fashion in East Mission Road H.S. She remembered the high school football games on Friday nights. She was a cheerleader and had a close friend named Martha who also made the squad. The two of them and the rest of the squad would join the football team on the sidelines before the game. Coach Miles would kneel down on one knee and all the kids would surround him. Every start of every game the coach, the squad and the team would say a prayer. Nobody said anything negative about the prayer and the kids looked forward to it. Today they couldn't do that and she couldn't understand why. Maybe she did understand, but she just couldn't imagine that anyone would truly try to kick God out of any part of their life. Yet it was happening at her old high school and she wanted it to stop.

It was her want, her desire, her mission to stop this insanity. Somehow she was bound and determined to have an effect on those people on the board and the superintendent. She thought that there may be one person or maybe two in the group who didn't really agree with the way things were going and may be able to change the direction of the others. She thought she understood the power that she was going up against. The members of the Nazarene congregation, who weren't on their way to the meeting, were in prayer at the church to lend spiritual aid in this fight about to begin. It was the best ammo the small army of church members had to stand up to "the powers that be" and the power that supported them.

She turned left into the parking lot of the school. The evening sun was going down below the horizon and silhouetted the almost black school with the beautiful setting rays of yellow and red. She saw that there was a parking place open to the left of the entrance she was going to use to get to the meeting room. She pulled in and turned off the engine of her Dodge Durango. She didn't get out right away but looked around the lot to see if any of her church team had arrived. The time was 6:45pm. The meeting was scheduled to start at 7:00pm.

Tom Hennessey and his wife Barbara were sitting in the white Ford pickup truck waiting for others to arrive or maybe Dee Dee herself. Grandpa Bob and Grandma Silvia, as the entire Nazarene congregation called them, had just pulled into the lot behind her and were parking next to her. Philip and Bobby Smith, the brother students had borrowed their dad's big, black Lincoln and were slowly, deliberately and carefully driving as they parked in the lot. The whole team was there or arriving as she stepped out of her SUV and waited for some of her small army to join her so they could enter the school together. Tom and Barbara were the first ones to do so.

There were hugs exchanged as more of the group gathered outside the door. "Let's do this." Dee Dee said and grabbed the cold handle of the door, swinging it open wide enough so many of the group could enter at the same time. All fifteen members who had said they would be there were, in fact, and they were confident that the other members were also doing their part in a prayer service at the church.

Room 124 was used only for meetings. It was set up with three 10 foot folding tables on the back side of the room as you enter. Chairs were placed on the other side of the tables for those who ran the meetings. There were approximately 30 other chairs placed in front of the three tables to provide seating for those who would be attending. There were two microphones in the meeting room, one in the center of the center table and the other on a stand located in the middle of the floor in front of the chairs provided for the audience. The standing microphone was intended for the use of anyone who wanted to address the members of the board at this or any other meeting.

The word must have gotten out about Dee Dee's mission this evening because there were an unusual number of individuals in attendance, all seated in the audience chairs in random fashion. Dee Dee's group all sat together once they had entered the meeting room. Dee Dee took a chair that would allow her easy access to the microphone and tried to settle into a comfortable position placing the legal pad, which had her notes, on her lap. She looked around the room and tried to determine if the people whom she didn't know may be there to support the church's position and therefore would be in support of her too. She couldn't tell from their faces if she was right or not. It was almost 7:00pm and there were more people coming in the door, taking the last of the available chairs. Soon there would be only standing room. She again hoped that the late arrivals were a good sign.

When the gavel was hammered down on the wooden stand, calling the meeting to order by the board chairman, the room was packed with half of the attendees standing in the rear of the room and along the walls to the right and left of the audience chairs. She and her fifteen companions were outnumbered but she felt confident that the majority of those who arrived for this meeting were looking for the same conclusion as she.

The chairman of the board was Bill Johnson, a man she didn't know other than in his position as the chairman and then only from the newspaper and television reports of the board activities. He had the look of a business man. He could have been a lawyer or a doctor taking on the responsibility of the school business. He was dressed in a white shirt and tie. There was a suit jacket draped over the back of his chair. Only one of the other six board members was dressed in that formal manner and that was the superintendent himself. Claude Millard was the picture of what a superintendent should look like. He could have been cast in the role of "Mister Peepers" the old television show, staring Wally Cox.

Millard was still dressed in his suit coat complete with a vest.

The two women and the other three men had all been seated at the folding tables when Dee Dee came into the meeting room. She didn't know any of them, except for Millard, probably because none of them had been interviewed by the media.

One of the other men looked familiar to her. She had probably seen him in the grocery store or other public place. She was ready to meet them all, head on.

Bill Johnson asked for the minutes to the last meeting to be read into record. Then Johnson read some of the old business that needed to be addressed and reported on it. This process took about one half hour. Johnson then asked for new business. Dee Dee was going to stand up when one of the other individuals in the room, whom she didn't know, stepped up to the microphone to ask about the price being raised for the noon lunches provided by the school. He stated that his name was Gary Wilburn and that he had three sons in the grade school. His point was that the increase of the cost of the meal would put a burden on his family and he couldn't justify the reason that they would have such a large increase of $1.00 all at one time rather than in gradual steps. He could budget for a small increase over a period of time but the dollar was too much.

Johnson told him that the board would take his concerns under consideration and would address the subject at a later time. Gary Wilburn was not happy with that answer and told the board, "What kind of answer was that. You raised the price of the lunch without any of us knowing about it and now you won't give us an opportunity to voice our objection." Johnson responded, "We just heard your voice, Mister Wilburn and now we will discuss it." Wilburn told him, "Discuss it right now so we can all hear what you say and so you can hear what we will say." Some of the attendees mumbled in agreement with Wilburn. Johnson told all of them, "We will discuss this at a later time. It was not on the agenda for this meeting." Wilburn started to object again but Johnson hammered the gavel again and told the audience he would clear the room if the meeting got out of order. Wilburn, defeated, left the microphone and the room, slamming the door behind him. A couple of the other members of his party left with him all making comments under their breath about how the board was operating business like the Mafia. The room of visitors became uneasy with the situation and the visible signs of their discomfort were obvious. There was shifting in their chairs. There was whispering going on to one another. The board members were equally aware of the room's change in atmosphere and were also shifting in their chairs as they whispered to each other.

The microphone stood alone waiting for someone to join it to change the feeling in the room that was so obvious to all in attendance. Dee Dee stood up and walked the short distance to the waiting voice enhancer, cleared her voice and spoke to the board.

"With some interest I have followed your continuing efforts to remove, from our schools, any reference to religion or spirituality. Your first action, as reported in the newspapers and on television was to remove particular books from the school library. This is not acceptable in the United States of America. We are neither the Soviet Union nor Hitler's Germany. We don't burn books here. We didn't say anything when you did this horrible deed and I regret that. I regret that we didn't come here before tonight because maybe we could have stopped your continuing campaign to remove God from our children's lives. You think that you have the power to take our children and put atheist thoughts in their minds. Do you think you have any real power that doesn't come from our Creator? If that is your thoughts then you are falling off the deep end of a bridge that you have built yourselves.

I came here tonight with fifteen other Christians to try to stop this board from taking another step down your dark pathway. This room is full of people that I believe are in complete harmony with our mission to correct the Anti-God effect that you seven people are pushing into our schools. Just like the man before me, Mr. Wilburn stated, we have not been heard on these matters and we are all here tonight to be heard and we will not leave this building until you listen to us and do something to correct the mistakes you have already made."

She took a breath and looked around the room to see if she had the support of the people in the room other than the group she came in with. There was not a sound to be heard. Not the drop of a pin. Not the whispers that had been mouthed before. She saw the approving glances on the faces of the fifteen church members first then she saw the faces of the others. She didn't understand, at first, what she was seeing in their eyes. She misunderstood the facial features that were apparent to everybody else in the meeting. In her adrenaline rush, provided by the speech she had prepared and now given, she expected that all there would be in perfect unison; this is what she wanted to see. She was wrong.

The two high school boys Phil and Bobby were the first ones who recognized the evil stares coming from the eyes of the other people. There was a deep hatred visibly presented in the fiery, red, blazing orbs of the individuals standing all around the fifteen representatives from the church. It was not a natural or normal sight that the boys saw and they were frightened. Soon other church members, one by one caught the looks on the faces of those around them. As each church member saw the eyes, their fright began to change to terror. The cold silence made the situation almost unbearable to stay in the room. Then the sounds started. It sent a chill up Dee Dee's back. It was a hissing sound, a very guttural bubbling that was followed by a strong spitting hiss. It was emanating from the non-church goers but yet it was not coming from any one of them. It was a combination of sounds bouncing off the walls and ceiling even coming from the floor. It permeated the room with a vile horrible sense of evil that the believers had never experienced. With equal speed the evil and the terror became the prominent emotions shared in the meeting room. The board members never changed expression; never spoke a word as if they had never heard a word of the prepared speech nor were aware of the change now present throughout the room.

Barbara Hennessey made a break for the door with her husband following in close order. Neither made it to the door. The evil group completely surrounded both of them almost immediately. They surrounded the man and wife yet no one touched either of them. Tom and Barbara sank to their knees and were both reeling with the pain that had consumed their bodies. Barbara was shrieking so loud that the horrible hissing was drowned out. Tom too was screaming from the pain and soon fell over unconscious. Barbara followed her husband to the floor and laid there beside him in the same condition. The boys were the next to break for the exit in the state of panic. Philip & Bobby didn't get as far as Tom and Barbara in their attempt to get away. Both of the young men fell immediately to their knees and immediately became unconscious. The rest of the group that had accompanied Dee Dee to the school fell to the floor, where they were standing, all in the state of unconsciousness.

Dee Dee was now the only one of her group that stood untouched by whatever evil force was active in that room. "What are you people doing to my friends?" She yelled at Johnson but meant it for everyone in the room. She was scared out of her wits and the question came from her out of fear more than from her need for an answer. Still there was no response from anyone on their feet. The sound of the guttural hissing became even more present to her. It wasn't louder; it just seemed to get deeper into her being, so much so that just the sound was beginning to give her pain. Although none of the people in the room had paid her much attention up until now, all their attention had suddenly shifted to her and she could feel their blazing, fiery eyes looking deep into her skull with extreme hatred. She almost passed out from just their intense stares.

It was Johnson who finally spoke. "Bitch, you will not dictate any of your garbage to us. We do not want your God anywhere near our children. You will take your slimy, vile friends away from our schools and never return. We will take care of the children. Leave now!" There was no doubt in her mind that she was leaving right this instant but she wondered and worried about how her friends were going to leave with her. She had been commanded and the horror of the night left her no choice. She had to go. She turned to leave from what had been the front of the audience near the microphone that was now the rear of where everybody was standing and her friends were on the floor. Dee Dee took one step and felt the explosion of pain that radiated from her right leg as the femur broke in two. She cried out in pain, staggered forward trying not to fall catching her balance and putting all her weight on her left leg. Her hands went out to assist in her attempt to balance and clamped on the tops of two chairs previously occupied by the Grandpa Bob and Grandma Silvia but were now vacant. As soon as she had her balance her left femur broke and another immense pain surged through her body and she went directly to the floor crying loudly from the pain and fear that had completely taken over her being.

Withering and reeling in agony, she was nearing unconsciousness when Dee Dee felt a strong hand on her shoulder, placed there in an effort to comfort her. The hand belonged to Tom Hennessey who had regained his senses the moment Dee Dee's right leg broke. The other church members also regained consciousness at the exact moment of her pain. Together most of the fifteen lifted her from the floor. Some of them could only help by verbally encouraging her to "Hang in there, Kiddo." They were successful in getting her out of the school and the teens directed the adults to put her in the back seat of the Lincoln. The boys would drive her to the hospital and the others could follow in their vehicles. Tom got the keys to Dee Dee's SUV from her purse and drove the Dodge to the hospital. Tom's wife Barbara drove their truck. At the hospital Tom called

Dee Dee's husband, Thomas and tried to explain what had happened at the school with little success. He hardly knew how to explain something that he didn't understand, something so unnatural and frightening. He did his best and Thomas told him that he would be at the hospital as soon as possible.

The church members, who were not in the emergency room with Dee Dee, when Thomas arrived, were in the waiting room, all in prayer. He ran to her side and she smiled through the tears and the medication that had been pumped into her veins to help reduce the terrible pain of two broken legs. She tried to tell him what happened but it wasn't making any sense to him. He would catch up on what had occurred soon enough. The doctors were getting ready to take her to surgery and he would be able to talk more with the group then. She kept telling him over and over, "There was no support! There was no support from Him!" He didn't understand. None of them understood. They didn't understand why the prayers of all the church members weren't heard. They just didn't understand.

CHAPTER FOUR

THE BACKYARD GARDEN

The garden in the backyard was more important to her than her own kids. That was what her husband Jess told her on more then on one occasion. Jess' real name was Willard but many years ago there was a famous boxer named Jess Willard so the nickname Jess caught on when he was a young man and it stuck. It was true that the garden, tomatoes in particular, was very much a part of her life but So were the four kids; two boys, one a Catholic priest and then two girls that they had raised and now had gone their own ways. Jess would never have said that the garden was more important than the grandkids, that would have caused a fight and they hadn't had a fight in over twenty years. The garden took a lot of time. It started with Jess early in the spring tilling the soil and adding what was given to him by her to enrich the black dirt. Sometimes it was horse manure; sometimes it was the fertilizer she purchased from the Target store. There was always something to add even though he didn't always know what it was or where it came from. The tilling was the extent of his responsibilities with the garden even though she tried to solicit his help occasionally with the weed removal project later in the year.

Barbara would actually start the garden before Jess tilled it up by planting seeds in the small egg dividers of paper cartons they saved for that purpose. Jess had offered a number of years ago to build a green house attachment off the right side of the screened porch and Barbara had taken him up on the offer. She got so excited about the project, she found herself helping him so that the job could be completed before either had expected. The glass enclosure couldn't be used the first year, it was too late in the season, but it had been put to good use the following years without exception.

She was there in the greenhouse putting tomato seeds into the cartons and transplanting some of the seedlings into larger containers of Quick Grow when she first noticed the drastic change of weather outside. It had been snowing about 7:30am this morning when she got up and poured her first cup of coffee. Jess joined her about 8:00am in the kitchen and mentioned that the snow at this time of the year, which was early March, wouldn't last long. "If you don't like the weather in Kansas just wait 10 minutes." An old joke shared by anybody living in the center of the United State and for some un-laughable reason it was almost always a truism. Today was different. Barbara's forehead started the perspiration, and then she felt the droplets of sweat role down her back. It was 10:00am and the weather had changed. She looked at the outside thermometer. It showed 95 degrees. From snow to the tropics in two hours, even in Kansas was not to be believed. She walked out of the small enclosure into the backyard and the temperature was confirmed for her in the heat of the morning sun.

Jess joined her right away from the garage. "What the hell is going on?" he asked her. "Honey I don't know. I've lived here all my life and I have never lived through this before." Jess was from Minnesota but had moved here to the Midwest long before he had met Barbara. He definitely had never lived through this either.

They walked back into the greenhouse together. She turned on the exhaust fans and he opened some of the windows. They needed to get some of the sweltering heat out of the baby plant nursery before their growth was affected or they were killed by the sun's tremendous power. As soon as they were assured that they had done all they could do to protect the young plants Jess and Barbara went in the house, turned on the air conditioning and then the television.

The weather station was reporting as much confusion as they attempted to explain the huge change in temperature. It wasn't just in Kansas that this phenomenon was occurring but there was a line of an unusual cloud formation stretching from the northwest corner of panhandle of Texas all the way to the northeast corner of Wisconsin. The cloud formation was the only visual evidence of the tremendous change of weather experienced all along its way. The cloud formation presented an even more concerning situation for the Weather Bureau. It was impossible to explain why the temperature was hot under the clouds and seasonably correct where there were no clouds. The reality of clouds was exactly the opposite; they should shield the earth from the rays of the sun.

The next two days there was no change in the temperature night or day. The sun's disappearance in the west had no effect on the 95 degrees reported consistently all along the cloud formation. Barbara went out to the greenhouse a couple of time a day to make sure that the little young plants didn't wilt and die due to the high heat. The fan and open windows were not enough to control the constant deluge of heat in the small glassed room. Jess fixed a soaker hose above the table where the seed and seedlings rested. The hose then provided the constant drip that helped Barbara's precious prizes maintain life. They were doing all they could do to save the young plant lives.

Day three and it was over. When they woke up the morning of the fourth day, Barbara first of course, went down to the kitchen poured a cup of coffee and felt a chill. She shivered and checked the thermostat. It showed that the temp in the house was 62 degrees. For the last three days the temp in the house stayed at an uncomfortable 78 degrees and that they couldn't change no matter what they tried. They slept with no covers and a fan full blast. Neither of them slept well. The 95 degrees was not unusual for Kansas but for some reason this hot box created by the constant cloud cover was relentless and had a persistent effect on not only the temperature, but the behavior of the people who were enduring it. In the three days they had endured the heat, Jess and Barbara jabbed at each other with sharp words neither had intended, and became sorry for immediately afterwards.

This morning changed back to what it should have been all along. She adjusted the thermostat and turned on the small TV in the kitchen to the weather channel.

Jess had gotten cold with no covers, the fan on and the temperature back to normal. He struggled to stay sleeping until he realized what was wrong. He got out of bed and for the first time in the last four days, he put on his bathrobe. He joined his wife in the kitchen and almost without looking at the coffee pot filled his cup to the brim. He was intently watching the announcer explain the sudden disappearance of the clouds and the accompanying heat wave, unsuccessfully. It was apparent to anyone watching the program that he had no idea what had caused the problem or why it went away. Jess laughed at his lack of information, made a few funny comments and joined his wife at the kitchen bar. She made no indication to him that she had even heard his little bits of humor about a something she considered a very serious subject and found no humor in it.

Jess & Barbara, the community where they lived, the State of Kansas and the rest of the States eventually forgot about the strange occurrence of those early March days. The weather station stopped trying to explain something for which they had no explanation and the news networks made no mention of the clouds or the heat wave two days after it was gone. The weather turned nice about the end of April and Barbara was ready for her husband to do his thing with his garden responsibilities by April 24th.

With the soil ready by May 1st Barbara waited for the first full moon to plant the garden with all the young seedlings that made it to spring from the greenhouse. Planting time was around the corner. She had successfully saved numerous plants from the sweltering heat of March. Those plants included: tomatoes, carrots, bell and jalapeño peppers, radishes, lettuce, cabbage, cucumbers, onion sets, egg plant, zucchini, basil, parsley and dill. She always planted marigolds around the garden to discourage the rabbits from feasting on the goodies. There was going to be a lot to do on planting day but she was anxious to get the job done.

Early on the morning of May 4th Barbara had her work gloves in hand when she walked out of the greenhouse. She retrieved the bucket containing her garden tools and knee pads from the garage and picked up the potato eyes and onion sets from a box just outside the garage door. She made her way to where the garden had been for years and where Jess had tilled the soil again for her planting pleasures. It was an easy walk, about 20 yards from the house and 20 yards from the garage, centered in the back yard. They had a large yard full of decorative trees. All around the house were full of flowers that had been planted by Barbara over the years, mostly when the kids were little. The kids are raised and gone now. The house contained only the two of them but the flowers remained, some of them beginning to pop through the beds, some already bloomed and others in between.

Barbara dropped her gardening supplies near the garden's edge. She went back to the greenhouse and loaded the small cart with the little containers of little plants none of them having seen the outside world yet. Gently she placed each egg carton on the cart with a touch of motherly love and care. Soon the cart held as many as possible and she moved them to their new home in the middle of the back yard. She knew better than to try and take all of the young seedlings to the garden at one time. Although she had all day to do the planting, she wasn't as young as she used to be and knew she would wear out before all the planting was complete. It was her back that would give out first even if she gave it a break a couple of dozen times during the day. It was the bending over that would do it. Once at the garden, she took each carton of seedlings to the particular row she had chosen for them to spend the summer and into the fall. Each row was designated with a paint stick that she had collected for as long as she could remember. She had marked the sticks with the name of the vegetable or tuber in that row. Each carton also had the name of the seedling marked with the same magic marker the day she planted the seed. The next step in the planting process for Barbara was to start on one end of the garden and work her way to the other. She always chose to work from her left to her right. There was no valid reason for that procedure but it suited her just fine and she always knew where her tools were while working in that direction and she was right handed.

Barbara knelt down on the pads, pulled the carton marked cabbage closer to her and removed the first of this year's seedlings. She really didn't need to use any of the garden tools, her fingers would have done the job in the loose soil but Jess had spent the time and money to purchase a very nice matched set of tools that included an extremely small shovel, a hoe and a rake. The set was a very well made miniature set of tools anybody would be proud of showing off at any opportunity, and she did. She dug the shovel into the dirt and placed the seeding in the hole, pushed dirt around the plant and firmly pushed it into place making sure no air would get to the roots and kill the plant. She measured down the row to where the next seeding would be placed into the ground and repeated the process. It took her about 15 minutes before the first row was completed and all the cabbages were happily planted in their new home. The paint stick marked CABBAGE was pushed into the ground at the end of the row. She went right away to the next row and started putting the carrots into the rich soil. At the end of the row she placed the appropriate stick in the dirt. The process, that was so familiar to her after all the years, continued until noon. At that time she had planted not only the cabbage and the carrots but two different kinds of peppers, the very small radish plants, the potato eyes and zucchini. Each plant was separated by the proper distances from each other and the other rows. Year of experience had given her a perspective on each plant's growth so it was easy for her to see into the future and visualize the zucchini, and potato's individual space needs. She got up from her kneeling position a couple of time since she started, to stretch her back but this time she not only stretched but went in the house to make lunch for the two of them.

Jess was watching the noon news on channel 5. He would watch only that station for the news, all the other news reports had too much talking between the commentators and the weather predictions were not as accurate as on channel 5. The weather reporter, named Brian, was predicting a gentle rain for tomorrow, starting about 10:00 am and continuing until about 9:00pm. When Jess told Barbara the report, she grinned a big toothy smile. Her timing had been perfect. She didn't need to express her happiness to him, he fully understood. She fixed two grilled cheese sandwiches using two kinds of cheese accompanied by two bowls of tomato soup, an all-time American favorite lunch. She took a break after lunch to let the slight pain in her back ease somewhat before returning to the joy of gardening. She told Jess about each row and how well it went including the part about stretching her back. She explained the slight pain in her back and he attempted to stall her from returning to the back yard so soon with no success at all.

Her next garden row was ready and waiting when she returned to the back yard. This time as she knelt down to start the after lunch planting, a song by John Denver came to mind and she started singing to herself. "Inch by inch, row by row, I'm going to make this garden grow. All it takes is a rake and a hoe and piece of fertile ground. Inch by inch row by, someone bless the seed I sow, someone warm them from below, 'til the rain comes tumbling down." She found a certain pleasure in all of Denver's songs but the first time she heard the Garden Song it found a special place in her heart and it was unusual that she wasn't singing it at some time while she was in the garden, especially in the spring while planting.

The last row was now in front of her and it was the special tomato row. She had always selected the three most popular varieties to start with: the Big Boy, the Big Girl and the Italian odd shaped tomato. From the basic three she expanded to a yellow and then the little salad tomatoes that Jess really liked. She was intrigued by the name Gargantuan and would give that new one a try as well. The tomatoes were planted and stakes pushed into the ground next to them in preparation for their growth. Later in the week she would take another half day and put in the pickle cucumbers, the squash and egg plants. She had always recruited Jess when planting the marigolds around the perimeter of the garden plot and this year would be no different. The flowers smelled bad to her and although they mostly did their job of keeping the critters out, she really didn't like working with them. When they were finally in the ground and Jess had done his yearly duty of planting, she always saw their yellow, orange and red beauty that added to the wondrous look of the garden. When it was complete she took a long admiring look at what had been accomplished and thought of what would come from the labor of her own hands and the hands of her wonderful husband. She was happy.

It was in June, the 12th of June exactly when she first noticed them. At first she thought they were ladybugs. They would eat the aphids. That would be great if that what was happening. Generally, to have ladybugs in the garden was a blessing and she would have smiled broadly at their presence. There was no smile on her face.

If they were in fact ladybugs, they weren't the kind she had ever seen before. They were devouring the plants and not any aphids. They were Jess's rose bushes; he had planted them, cared for them, and pruned them. They grew big and beautiful because he loved roses. They were on the big red Abraham Lincoln that was in full bloom where she saw the evidence of the ladybug eating the flower. She looked closely to determine if the insects were a Japanese beetle or a ladybug even though she knew that neither beetle would chow down on a rose normally. It was a ladybug and that knowledge made her even more concerned. What would have made the beetle start eating plant life? She went into the house and told Jess what she had seen. He jumped up from the easy chair where he was watching TV and went immediately out the front door to check out his pride and joy.

He was more than a little bit upset. There was evidence that the bugs were eating more than just the one rose that Barbara had told him about. He looked closely at the beautiful Peace rose, and the magnificent bright yellow one whose name he forgot. The bugs, as he called them, were on all the rose bushes and eating not only the flowers but the leaves and stems too. Aggravated and determined, he went immediately to the garage and searched the shelves for the dusting powder he used on occasion that was designed to rid the beautiful roses of these harmful pests. He read the instructions on the box trying to see if the powder would take care of a ladybug infestation. It wasn't there. He didn't care, the powder was going to be poured on his roses and it would kill the bugs that were eating them. If the powder didn't do the trick he would find a product that would.

Jess took the killing powder to the front of the house and gave the bugs a thorough dusting. Then he carefully watched to see the effect of the killing agent. He watched for one half hour precisely and at the end of that half hour not one bug dropped from the roses. Not one bug stopped eating. Not one bug showed any effect whatsoever of the powder. Jess grabbed the keys to the Chevrolet and drove to the local garden store, with only one thing in mind. He was going to kill the bugs.

He could find nothing that named ladybugs as a pest worth killing. He took what the salesman suggested was the strongest of all the products designed to kill insects. It was in a liquid form so he thought it might do a better job than what the powder had done. He drove directly home, got the hose off of the hanger, attached the spray bottle he located on the work bench to the hose and filled the bottle with the deadly concoction. He dragged the hose around to the front of the house where he found Barbara in tears. She was on her knees trying to pick the little insects from the roses and place them into a glass jar. Her fingers were bleeding and the tears that flowed from her eyes were there because of frustration and an equal amount of pain caused by not only the thorns piercing the skin but from the bites she was receiving from the ladybugs. She knew the love her husband had for the beautiful flowers and she wanted to do as much as she could to save the roses from this infestation.

Little did she know that her efforts were going to cause so much pain? She never suspected that a ladybug would bite much less draw blood and cause such pain.

Jess gently put his hands on her shoulders and lifted her from the kneeling position, turned her around and hugged her tightly. She sobbed into his loving arms. He then took her hands into his looking at the blood still seeping from the punctures and bites. He pulled the unused handkerchief from his back pocket and wrapped her right hand. It was the worst of the two. He kissed her on the forehead and sent her inside.

Now with an increased vengeance he turned the hose on and sprayed the roses where the little devils had taken up residence and were eating their homes. He sprayed for a long time, directly at the bushes with hatred in his heart. He let the spray fall over every part of the bushes. He sprayed under the leaves from a kneeling and bent over position that must have looked comical to anyone driving by. The bushes were completely soaked and the ground was saturated with the water- poison mixture. When the mixture was gone from the bottle he turned off the hose and took a very close look to see what effect the spraying had on the pests. Some had dropped to the wet mulch that surrounded the rose's base and were not moving. Some were still on the plants but they too had ceased movement. Perhaps the newly purchased bottle of killer fluid had done the job. Jess didn't smile but felt a certain amount of pleasure that he had taken care of the insect problem that was attacking his roses. He went in the house, after putting up the hose in the garage, to join his wife. Barbara had put an antiseptic on the cuts and punctures in her hands and was still bandaging the worst of the wounds when Jess came into the kitchen. He expressed his gratitude and sympathy for her efforts and admonished her for the same. He loved her too much to see her in so much pain and told her so. They went to bed early that night in each other's arms and slept peacefully until the break of dawn.

As usual Barbara was the first out of bed, went immediately to the coffee pot and then to the front of the house. As she opened the front door and went out to the porch, her legs collapsed and she went to her knees. The coffee in her cup spilled on the front porch as the cup itself broke when it fell from her hand. The rose bushes, that two days ago were full of green leaves and gorgeous blooms, were now nothing more than stems of thorns sticking out of the ground containing little holes that had been gnawed through by the ladybugs. Not one beetle appeared on what was left of the bushes. The Japanese Yews that were planted at the corners of the front of the house had become their next target. The beautiful chartreuse pine like leaves were almost nonexistent as the trees had been decimated by the bugs. Barbara just sat on the front porch looking at the tragedy in front of her home that had happened so quickly and again let the tears fall down from her eyes to her cheeks. Jess arrived at the porch, and saw what his wife had viewed before him. He left her there crying.

When he came back within a very few minutes he carried a propane torch in one hand and a stick with a rag, soaked in kerosene, wrapped around one end. He was ready to inflict as much damage as humanly possible to the beetles that had destroyed so much in such a short time. He lit the torch and then the rag on the stick. He pushed the flaming stick into the small tree. What happened next surprised both Jess and Barbara. As soon as the flame hit the Yew, all of the ladybugs took flight, and in a swarm circled the house, flew straight up into the air and disappeared.

After the swarm of ladybugs disappeared the rest of the summer went by with nothing unusual. The rose bushes were replaced and the process of Jess nurturing the young plantings started a new. The Japanese Yews died and Jess replaced them as well.

The beetles had touched nothing else in the yard so the garden was in good shape by September. Barbara continued to work as much as she liked, to help the vegetables, tubers and spices gain in strength and size. She liked being in the garden almost every day. She fed plant food and removed any weed or grass that tried to gain entrance to her domain. The potatoes had bloomed; the squash flowers were big and beautiful. The spices were being used in the kitchen daily and all was well in the world of Barbara's garden.

September 19th, two days after a nice gentle rain came-a-calling on the garden, Barbara with coffee cup in hand, walked her regular pathway to take the regular morning look at her produce in the ground. There was something funny. Something unusual there that she hadn't noticed before. The rain must have done something to the plants, even the tubers and vines. They didn't look real. The leaves appeared to be made of plastic. The stems looked like they were wrapped wire. There was no shine on the leaves, even after the rain, that should have cleaned off any dust that would have prevented a shine that is evident on healthy plants. Could it have been something present in the rain that did the opposite of what a regular rain would do? Barbara was confused and concerned. She didn't take just a closer look; she got down on her knees without any pads and pulled up one of the carrots. It was not plastic but it wasn't a regular carrot in feel or look. She tried to bend it to make it break but it twisted into a complete circle, more so than if it had been out of the ground and not refrigerated for three or four days.

She dropped the carrot and went to the beets. There she discovered that the beets had been turned to mush and appeared to be made of a different unnatural substance foreign to her and the garden. She pulled three or four more beets from the ground and found them to be of the same repulsive material. The potatoes she had to dig in the ground to find. When she found them they were in the same situation as the other vegetables and tubers. She ran to the back of the house where she had planted the pickle cucumbers and found them to be rubbery.

She cried to no one asking the unanswerable questions, yelling the frustrations of her heart, screaming the terror of her discovery. Her emotions peaked and her heart started beating hard and fast. Jess heard the distressed calls coming from their back yard and with great concern, left the comfort of this recliner to run out of the house to his wife. He arrived in time to witness her collapse into the vines that grew the abnormal cucumbers. He rushed to her side, holding her in his loving arms and asking what the matter was. Through her tears and labored breathing he couldn't understand her words. "Where has God gone?"

CHAPTER FIVE

THE B.W.C.A

Larry had gone to the Boundary Waters Canoe Area of northern Minnesota the majority of his life. The first time he went north from Kansas City was as a Boy Scout. His father and their neighbor were the leaders and he was a 15 year old that year. Now in his mid 60's Larry still found every trip a cleansing experience for his soul. He had been raised a Catholic but somewhere in his younger adult life he dropped the church and all its teachings. His inquiring mind never stopped asking spiritual questions but he found answers in the sciences. He once told a friend that he believed the light seen by so many near death experienced people was nothing more than the brain shutting down and very similar to the light that appears on a television screen after turning that off for the night. So the cleansing that he so looked forward to was never a religious experience but more of a physical resting time he could only achieve there in the wilderness among nature's wonders.

The trips would always start very early in the morning allowing him to get to the Twin Cities late morning and Duluth by noon. The MacDonald's fast food stop was the first resting spot he allowed himself or his companions if someone had accompanied him to the BWCA. The restaurant located on the north side of the city was unusual in that it had a very large aquarium right in the middle of the building. It was always a welcome respite on this long journey to the northeastern tip of Minnesota called the arrow head where the town of Ely waited as his destination. Ely was the place where Larry would stop for the night before going into the area. He had met the owner of an outfitter lodge at the sports show in Kansas City many years ago and over the years had formed a friendship that allowed Larry very good pricing for the supplies he needed for the excursion. Larry would stay in the lodge, get up before dawn and take the same required instructional pre-trip session every time he entered the BWCA.

John, the owner of the lodge, was on the front porch as Larry pulled into the gravel parking lot. The lodge was built on the bank of the White Fish River, allowing a beautiful view of the scenery from the lodge's main dining room in the back of the huge building. Larry got out of his SUV and walked over to greet his friend and host John. They had not seen each other since Larry's fall trip last year. It was June now and still cool in the evenings and mostly in the high 50's during the day. The weather was perfect for a canoe trek. Larry purposely chose this time of the year, with the temperature in that range the bugs wouldn't be a problem. He might get into some early spawn activity with the smallmouth bass and enjoy a good shore lunch with a couple of them and a Northern or two.

John had set him up with two large knapsacks, one filled with food needed for four nights and five days in the wilderness and the other with his tent and sleeping requirements. The two bags, his cloths, fishing equipment and the canoe will be the only items Larry will take with him in the morning. Tonight he and John will enjoy each other's company over a plate of fresh walleye that Larry has been thinking about all day long.

Larry took his light bag of items to which he would later add to one of the large nap sacks, and deposited it in the small room he would use only tonight and again when he came out of the area the fifth day. He freshened up a little by splashing cold water from the sink in the bathroom, on his face and washed his hands. He changed his shirt and walked to the bar to have a whiskey and water before diner.

He had no more than finished the drink when John came to join him. John had quit drinking years ago. He had been a top salesman for Honeywell and it was almost required that he took a client to the bar and keep up with them until the deal was signed. He had drank too much during those pressured times so when he had the opportunity to buy the lodge he grabbed it and dropped the alcohol at exactly the same time. His life style changed and so did his blood pressure. The hardest part of running the lodge and outfitter business was traveling with the sports shows but that in comparison to what he had done as a salesman was a cake walk. It was at the Boat Sports & Travel Show in Kansas City at the Municipal Auditorium that he and Larry had first met. When Larry approached John's booth and asked him about his facility and what he could supply for a trip into the BWCA not only were the answers appealing to Larry but so was this fun and friendly man named John. So it began fifteen years ago.

John and Larry sat in the dining room, Larry looking out at the beauty of the river and John paying little attention to a sight he had become used to. Larry inquired about the fishing in the area and John reported that there was little activity he was aware of reported by his clients upon their return from the wilderness. This lack of information concerned Larry. He had always gotten some type of success story from John, about the fishing in some parts of the vast chain of lakes in the BWCA, from his clients upon their return. Larry had particular camp areas in the area that were favorites and part of the reason was the success he had throwing a plug or spoon. To think that no one had reported back to John of a successful fishing trip was unthinkable. He pressed John on the subject but the answer remained the same. No report of a positive experience.

Larry's dinner of fried walleye pike almondine was finished and he sat back in the comfortable dining room chair, stretched and considered the bread pudding for dessert. John told him that the bags were already packed for the trip and he had included the usual T-bone steak, still frozen, for the first nights dinner at the camp site. That was something John would do for only a few of his special clients and Larry knew the steaks were put in the bag just for him. Larry also found out from John that there was a restaurant in Ely that would take an order for a lobster dinner to be enjoyed by someone the evening they came out of the area. Larry hadn't taken opportunity of enjoying that delicacy but decided at dinner to do so. He made mental note to call the Chocolate Moose before going to bed that night. He was on vacation. Why not indulge? Larry ordered the bread pudding complete with the brown sugar sauce and enjoyed it to the fullest.

When dinner with John was over Larry walked out to the end of the dock that extended over the river to take in more of the early evening grandeur of the northern, forest wilderness even though it was in the city of Ely. Many places in Ely you could escape the city in just a few steps and he did just that. He watched the water moving with some speed, past where he stood from the left to the right of the dock and beneath his feet as he stood there in the dusk. He was breathing in a place that held more than a little charm in his eyes and in his heart. He tried to get himself to the dock in the dusk every visit to the lodge. Most of the time he was able to do that very thing and when he didn't it bothered him a little.

When he could no longer see the other side of the river because of the fading light, he walked into the main room of the lodge where he knew a pay phone was located. He could have used his cell phone to make the call but the reception in Ely was questionable at the least and disconnecting at the worst. He put a quarter in the slot and dialed the familiar number to the Chocolate Moose. "I'd like to order a live Maine lobster for dinner when I come back from my canoe trip." Larry requested when the phone was answered. "I'm sorry sir; we can't fill that order. We have not been able to get lobster delivered for about a month now." was the answer. Curiosity got the best of Larry and he asked, "Why not?" The lady on the other end of the line told him, 'They haven't been able to trap any for some time now. They think it might be the global warming that has affected the lobster catch. Sorry Sir."

Larry's disappointment was temporary, he had been let down by more important things in his life and now being past 40 years of age, the loss of a lobster dinner was not an issue. He walked to his room and prepared to get up before the birds tomorrow morning. Sleep was not going to come easy because of the anticipation he felt every time he was going to enter the wilderness again. The trek was always an adventure, always different, always special in some way and how he did love it.

The alarm went off at exactly 4:00am.and Larry woke from a deep sleep surprised that he had fallen asleep at all. He refreshed himself, put on his wilderness cloths, grabbed his personal back pack and walked out the door into the dark of the new day yet to be defined by any light. The exterior lights were on all over, illuminating the outside of the lodge especially the area that Larry knew he had to join the gathering permit holders some of whom were already in place. There was a poured slab about 20' X 20' with a wooden roof held up by 6"X 6" pillars which was their destination that early morning. The single bulb hanging from the center of the roof was enough to light the area below. When all the rest of the individuals, who were entering into the BWCA that morning, were standing on the slab, one of the young men who worked for John started the rehearsed speech given so many times to so many people before they ventured into the wilderness. The instructions and rules had been heard at the beginning of every trip Larry had taken and was as much of the part of the trip as sitting in the canoe and putting the paddle in the water.

The large knap-sacks had been assigned to the people going in the area, and were being given out accordingly. Larry's big bag was placed in front of him and he immediately opened the top of the canvas container placing his personal items in with the items provided by John. When he did this he saw the frozen steaks that John had personally placed in his sack. Larry grinned to himself. He enjoyed and appreciated the benefits of his friendship with John.

Three canoes were placed on top of the SUV and the back hatch was opened up so the bags that would accompany them could be put inside. Larry and two other people were instructed to get into the older but very reliable Ford when it was fully packed. Larry introduced himself to Jay and Molly. The two kids were going into the wilderness on their honeymoon. When Larry learned this he again smiled to himself. Going into the BWCA on a honeymoon would not have even been discussed by his wife of 35 years. As of this day Doris has never had any interest in venturing into any wilderness much less to the area that truly defines the meaning of the word. Larry got into the front passenger's side next to John and the two honeymooners kissed as they got into the back seat.

The drive to Lake One was a short 15 minutes and they were there. Larry got out first and started getting the canoe nearest to him off the roof of the SUV. He knew what to do and what not to do in an effort to assist John before putting into the water. Jay helped Larry and the two of them placed both canoes at the water's edge. John had removed the big backpacks and placed them near the canoes. Larry didn't wait for the two kids. He placed his bags in the canoe he chose and pushed the nose of the boat into the water. Having done this 100 times before helped him ease into the craft with little effort. He pushed the bottom of the canoe off the rocks with the paddle and was moving along at a good pace even before the kids were in their canoe.

The sun was up in the east, lighting the water and surrounding pine forest with a beautiful orange and pink hue before him. His effortless paddling of the "J" stroke moved his canoe along the water path he had chosen even before starting the long drive to Minnesota. Each trip he had taken to the BWCA was a little bit different and this one was no exception. He would put-in at Lake One, as he had done before, but he choose different campsites and portages for this trip. His first portage was about an hour's distance from the put-in site and was coming up sooner than he had anticipated. He must have been moving faster than he thought. There was no wind to contend with and thus the travel was a straight line and faster. He eased the bow into the rocks on the shore of the first portage and then moved the left side of the craft into the shore rocks. It was an easy thing to put the big bag on the shore and exit soon after. He grabbed the shoulder bar and pulled the boat out of the water. There was a Jack Pine with limbs cut off except for one fairly sturdy one up the tree about ten feet. Larry placed the bow of the boat on the limb and retrieved the backpacks. Once on his back he moved under the canoe and lifted it off the limb and started walking the short portage.

As he topped the little hill and prepared to descent the other side of his portage he accidentally stepped on a canadian jay. The bird crunched under his weight but made no other sound. Larry hoped that it was dead before he had tromped on it. In fact he was sure that it had already met its demise. He couldn't possibly imagine that he could have stepped on a live bird. It just wasn't possible. He then looked up from that disturbing sight of the smashed bird and saw something equally disturbing. As he looked around the moss covered floor of the forest he saw live birds of various breeds just sitting there. As far as his eyes could see in the morning light, he saw the birds. Some were medium sized birds like evening grosbeaks, cardinals and jays. Others were smaller species like the winter birds called juncos, some sparrows, the little gold finches and purple finches. There were birds of prey sitting there also like the red tailed hawk, the sharp shinned hawk, a couple of great horned owls and a few young bald eagles not yet in the white head feathers of an adult. None of the birds were moving. They just sat there as if they had been hypnotized by some evil magician.

Larry found a tree similar to the jack pine on which he first rested the canoe and again placed the canoe. He got out of the backpacks and walked towards one of the eagles being careful not to step on any of the other birds in his pathway. He fully expected the large symbol of our Country to dodge his attempt to touch it but when he hunkered down and reached out to feel the feathers under his fingers, the bird didn't move an inch. Larry petted the big bird for a time before deciding to pick it up. He placed his left hand under the breast of the eagle and put his right hand on top. Gently he lifted the bird into his arms, cradling it close to his chest. He could feel the bird breathing and its heartbeat as he held it in that manner. It didn't seem sick in any way, just very distant in attitude.

Larry couldn't figure out what was happening but he knew that he didn't like it at all. He put the bird back down and carefully walked around other feathered creatures back to the canoe and backpacks.

All the way down to the shore line of the next body of water that he was going to negotiate, he saw the birds. Maybe it was something they were dusting with to kill unwanted vegetation that affected the birds? No that couldn't be, they didn't control like that in this wilderness area. Mercury poisoning maybe? How could that be? No, that wasn't likely either. He kept trying to come up with the answer to "why" but failed with each attempt. He was a thinker. He prided himself with his ability to study science and knew more than the average person about how things operated and the source of that operation. He had always been a man of never ending questions and the need to find those answers in nature. He could explain the star systems, the workings of the ocean floor, identify the different plant life that covered the earth and all the animal of the world. His love of the wilderness was so intense partially because he could examine the tiniest molecules in the sea and the largest star in the heavens to come up with the answers to the question of "why". The wilderness became a classroom where he found new subjects of science to study every day. All of his answers came exclusively from science.

There was no question that could not be answered with scientific answers. Larry was not a man of faith.

There was a time in his life when his Catholic upbringing meant something to him but that was long ago. The last time he entered a church was to bury his father. His mother was the only member of the family of two boys and two girls who still attended mass on a regular basis. Larry was a caring, good man who believed in the rights of every man and always treated everyone he knew with respect. He was living a life most Christians would only try to accomplish. So the answers he sought, even on this day, would never have a faith based solution.

He turned the canoe over and placed the bow into the water a move he had accomplished too many times to count but this time his mind was a million miles away from the water's edge. The birds were heavy on his mind. He couldn't figure out what had happened and the solution was no closer now than when he had first stepped on the jay. Placing the backpacks in the boat and getting in to start the next portion of his journey was accomplished without a thought of the procedure. He was on the water paddling "J" stokes before he realized he had even gotten into the boat. He stopped the canoe and with the same motion of the paddle, he turned it around to take one last look at the portage. Maybe it was all an illusion and he hadn't really seen anything unusual. He was wrong. The birds were all along the shore and up the trail, just sitting there as if in a stupor. He had to find out why.

Again the canoe was turned around and he marked his direction away from the shore and the birds with the compass he pulled from the breast pocket of his jacket. He tried to concentrate on the journey in front of him but the question kept disrupting his progress. The canoe cut through the surface of the lake leaving a little wake behind the craft as it was directed by Larry to the next portage on the opposite shore. Without knowing it, his eyes constantly searched the shore line looking for more birds in the same situation.

All along the shore he indeed did find the same thing that he had already experienced. The birds, not crowded, were all along the shore just sitting there. There was no movement, no aggression, and no interest that they showed in any thing around them. It was the most disturbing sight Larry had ever seen.

The short voyage to the opposite shore was over and he again maneuvered the bow of his canoe into the rocks on the shore, brought the boat's side close to the shore and placed the big backpacks on the rocks. He got out of the canoe, eyed the shore line and the thin woods of pine trees where the next portage started. It wasn't just the birds here that had no interest in their environment. Larry almost fell to his knees when he saw the rest of this daytime nightmare. Deer, fox, mink, squirrel, a big black bear all in the same type of stupor, just laying or standing in the open. This was so wrong. This was so very wrong. None of the animals moved away from the threatening presence of a predator or even the most deadly of all predators, man. Larry sat down on a big rock put his face in his hands and felt the heaviest weight descend upon his very being. The feeling was so strong it almost brought a man who never cried to tears. The emotions of the heavy weight were exploding inside of him.

He wanted to run as fast as he could away from what he was seeing in his beloved wilderness that made no sense to him. There was no answer, no reason, no logic and he had dove deep into his education of the wild things yet he sat on this big rock with depression totally consuming his mind no farther into solving the "WHY" than when he started.

Totally exhausted and emotionally drained he stood up and walked to the biggest animal in this part of the green forest. He was not even the slightest concerned for his well being. Larry had gone beyond that point and would have been surprised if the large animal have even growled at him. He had no intent. He just walked over to an animal whose presence he had never experienced in this close proximity without the safety of zoo bars of separation. With shaking right hand extended, he touched the glossy coat of deep black fur and when in contact with the animal Larry heard himself exhale the breath he didn't know he had drawn in and held. The bruin's head turned ever so slightly towards Larry not so much in an effort to stop the touch of Larry's hand but to draw an un-inquisitive blank stare not at all focused on the unusual happening of a human touch but more in the general direction of the human standing only inches away.

What was this that had affected all the wildlife in his little portion of paradise? It wasn't natural but it was now becoming extremely frightening. He wasn't afraid of the listless animals and sitting birdlife. He was afraid of what had made them that way. The thought of turning back and getting out of the BWCA was all but impossible. He had come too far into the area to make it half way back before it turned dark and he was now beginning to feel ill at ease out there in the dark. He needed to find a camp site and make it ready for the night that was ahead of him.

He got back into the canoe and started looking for a campsite along the shore of the lake he had originally wanted to pass through to the second portage on his trek this first day. He not only looked for a good campsite but he watched for the birds and animals. He wanted a site with the smallest amount of the disturbing array of wildlife in attendance. He saw a rock peninsula sticking out of the otherwise smooth shore line and took a long careful inspection of the site. There was only one large animal standing on the outcropping so he decided to land the canoe there and take an even better look around the site and at the wolf.

After getting the bags and himself out of the boat he walked carefully around the second largest carnivore in the forest. Just like the other animals, the wolf had no concerns about anything going on around it. The animal was blankly looking out over the lake at nothing. Evidentially the presence of the wolf must have had an effect on the other locals before the "Happening" because Larry didn't see as many 'blanked – faced" wildlife around his chosen place to spend the night as he had expected. He thought maybe they had taken refuge from the predator and therefore were nowhere to be seen right now. Yet that didn't make sense to him either because of the huge number of birds and animals he had seen, all in close proximity to each other, except for here on this rocky portion of the shore. Again questions with no answers.

Larry walked over to the wolf. It was a large gray and black male with accents of white around the eyes and muzzle as well as the chest. He was a truly beautiful animal and one of a species that Larry admired from afar, except today. Larry put his hand on the middle of the back and felt the luxurious coat that had another finer, thicker undercoat of fur. The wolf did nothing different than what he had expected. The touch of Larry's hand on his back was more intense for the touch-er than the touch-ee. Larry noticed just the slightest turn of the wolf's head in the direction of his assailant but no animosity directed at him.

Larry didn't want any wolf, no matter how docile, around the camp where he was going to be sleeping that night. He tried to move the animal away from the area where he planned on setting up his tent. Larry attempted to push it in the direction of the forest game trail that led away from the site he had chosen for his slumber though he doubted that he would sleep much when the sun went down.

Larry had to get around the back side of the animal and push him forward. The wolf didn't really resist Larry yet it seemed to have no intent on going anywhere so the effort of moving the animal was difficult. At one point Larry had to push the wolf up a little incline in the trail that neared the edge of a drop off that ended up in the lake. That is exactly what happened. The wolf lost his footing and tumbled off into the water below. Larry scrambled down the embankment and into the water after the fallen animal. He couldn't believe his eyes. The wolf sank! It just tumbled down into the water and sank beneath the surface of the lake, making no effort to stay afloat. Bubbles filled the circles that came about from the wolf breaking into the lake. Larry went into the water.

He reached down about three feet into the shallows attempting to grab the animal but failed in his first try. The wolf was rolling down the light grade of the rocky bottom into the darkness where he couldn't be easily seen. Larry went in after him this time paying no attention to getting his clothes wet. It was too late. He dove down as far as he could and made another grab at the descending canine but came up to get breath empty handed. The bubbles stopped and a feeling of guilt came over Larry like he had never experienced before. He sat down on the big rock and did something he had barely ever done before in his adult life. He cried.

After getting out of his wet clothes and into the plastic wrapped dry ones he had packed the night before, he started a fire. This campsite was not one that had been set up as a regular stopping off spot so there were no cut logs to use as chairs, no cleaned off place to set up a tent and no toilet set up back in the trees. He loved "roughing it" but he had been spoiled over the years with all the improvement to the BWCA. Tonight he will not be thinking about the improvements at all.

After finding an appropriate stick, he pulled out the t-bones that John had packed especially for him and stuck one of the big steaks on the pointed end. He placed the steak-ed stick in a larger forked stick that he had pushed into the ground. He then placed a rock on the steak-ed stick so the t-bone would not fall into the fire. He got the garlic, salt and pepper from the pack and seasoned the meat. He had filled his canteen with water he took from the middle of the first lake. He poured the cherry flavored Kool-Aid into the Sierra cup and then the water. He removed a potato from the bag, sliced it and put it into a camp skillet with some lard. After seasoning the potato he placed the skillet in the fire. He was not particularly hungry but the meat beginning to sear did smell good to him. Maybe he would be hungry by the time his meal was ready. Right now his stomach churned from what he saw today.

He struggled through the meal and cooked the second steak and put it in a plastic bag for tomorrow. He cleaned the pan and cup and packed everything away in the bag. He then removed the tent, cushion and sleeping bag. It took only a short time to set up the tent and ready it for the night. A few more large sticks were placed on the fire not so much for the warmth but for the light it produced. It was getting darker and the light helped him feel more secure in a place he had referred to as paradise for as long as he could remember.

His feelings were as wrong as the things he saw this day. He found a comfortable resting place and putting his back against the smooth surface of the big rock he had been sitting on and settled in until time for sleep.

His mind kept up a continuous barrage of possibilities to the strange happenings in this northern woods yet not one feasible answer came to him. The frustration of this situation alone was enough to cause him great distress but the visions of the birds and animals were manifesting themselves to an extreme as the light of the day faded to an engulfing darkness causing him to question if the dinner he had just consumed would stay with him.

The time now, before getting tired, did not offer him the relaxation he had experienced on all the other trips into the area and he laughed to himself because he knew this was not at all like any of the other trips.

He tried to relax his mind and think of anything else. The kids, his wife, his job as a general contractor and one or two of the customers who were very demanding; he tried to bring them all to mind in an effort to escape the unreal scenes that were haunting him. It was finally his grandkids that pushed out the distress of the day. His mind went to the two girls that his daughter had given him. They lived out of state so their visits were precious even though the frequency could have been more. His pride in their cute little statements, from out of the blue, could be seen by anyone who would be fortunate enough to hear them and he tried his best to provide that opportunity at every opportunity.

Larry was deep into remembering Granddaughter Rose's statement about the mailman bringing more than mail when her sister was born. She was sure that it wasn't a stork at all but a "special delivery" from the post office because she had put the words "delivery" and "special" together to explain her sister's arrival. Grinning for the first time today he looked to the sky as he often did when relaxing to appreciate all the wonders of the universe. That's when he saw the first one.

Not at all sure of what he had seen, he concentrated on another of the "billions and billions of stars" as Carl Sagan had said so many times, to affirm his suspicion. There it happened again, and then another one. One by one the stars that were now filling the evening sky were blinking out. They were disappearing from view in the northern sky. He stood up almost as if to get a closer look. One by one at a rate of about 5 a second they were burning out. The stars in the heaven were dying.

For the first time today Larry remembered that he had a cell phone in his jacket pocket. His mind had been so occupied with questions that he could not find the answers to that he had forgotten the simplest things like the phone. He dialed John at the lodge. While he waited for the connection and John to answer he looked up into the sky seeing the stars blink out of existence. John answered, "Whitefish River Resort, this is John." "John this is Larry. What the hell is going on?

The birds are wrong and animals are wrong and now the stars are going away. John, what's going on?" John told him, "I don't know Larry the whole town is crazy. There's thousands of fish floating down the river like a big kill has taken place but they are all alive, just floating there on the top. People are coming out of the BWCA with stories you wouldn't believe and are scared to death. The tourists are leaving in droves. The place is crazy, Larry. Are you coming out too?"

Larry's stomach turned over with every word John spoke and now lost all the dinner he had put into it earlier. "I don't understand. What's going on John? I've seen stuff here today that I can't figure out. Has the DNR done something to the area that would cause all this?" said Larry, trying to control his emotions. "The DNR and the

Game Warden have no idea what has happened any more than we do and they are getting the brunt of the accusations coming from both sides. The visitors and the locals both are blaming the departments and they are in the dark too." Larry asked him, "Where are you right now?" Larry should have known that John was on the same phone in the lobby of the lodge where he tried ordering the lobster. "I'm in the lodge's lobby area. Why?" "Have you looked up into the sky lately? Larry asked. "No! Why?" John sounded more concerned now. "Go outside and look up. Tell me what you see." John answered, "I can't I'm on the phone, you idiot." "Just drop the phone and go out. I'll wait until you return. Go out!" Larry could hear the phone drop and bang against the wall of the lobby. He could hear John's footsteps as he walked away from the phone to go outside. A short time later he heard John's return. "The sky is falling, said Chicken Little only this time it really is. Larry, get out of there and come in. I'm leaving this damn place as soon as I can but I'll wait for you. We've got to leave." Larry spoke slowly into his cell phone, "I can't leave tonight. I don't have a flashlight and there is nothing to light my way in the heavens now." Larry hung up and made another call to his wife telling her he would be home earlier than he had expected.

CHAPTER SIX

COPS

F rank stepped into the dark blue uniform pants, zippered and buttoned the fly while tucking in the lighter blue uniform shirt that had the American flag on one shoulder and the city patch on the other. He was at the "cop shop" getting out of his street clothes and into his uniform in preparation to start his shift. The locker room, where Frank was changing clothes, was full of male officers also getting ready for the night shift. He knew all thirty four of the men by first name and about half of the names of their wives. It was a small department in comparison to the other cities in the near vicinity. There were 400 police personnel employed, 200 of them were in uniform and of those 200 there were 150 on the street, men and women both. Frank worked the street and had been on the midnight shift for the full ten years of his service. When he strapped on his leathers, holstered his weapon and walked upstairs to join roll call, he assumed the persona of an authority figure and walked a little taller. He was proud of being one of the people who would put his life on the line in an effort to protect and help the innocents of his city.

Ten years on the street put Frank right in the middle of an unusual time in his career. He was definitely not a rookie any longer and the "Old Salts" hadn't truly accepted him into the cliques yet. There were 35 other members of that "red-headed step child club' who just didn't fit their square pegs into the round holes. All 35 members graduated the academy together. He found his usual place in the roll call room and took up residence in the usual chair next to Jerry Kuban. Jerry was a large, loud and somewhat intimidating individual who became a close friend over the years. Jerry his wife Pat, Frank and his wife Mary were social friends as well. Neither Frank nor Jerry liked the personalities of the majority of cops they knew. The other officers, with whom they worked, seemed to be of a particular mind set. That mind set was of arrogance and unquestioned authority. That personality was not something that the two wanted to be around off the job. Their desire to not associate off the job with the other officers was never present on the job so they both settled into their respective chairs to listen to the information given out to the members of the night shift by Sergeant Lopez. Juan Lopez reported to the shift commander Lt. Ward who very seldom appeared at roll call but was on the streets shortly after the fifteen to twenty minute information session given each night at 12:00am precisely.

Lopez told the waiting shift members that there had been an unusual number of calls received by the afternoon shift and all of them were violent in nature. The 4pm to midnight cops were busy from their roll call until the time when they should have been checking out to go home, yet most of them were in the report writing room still filling out their reports from the night.

Lopez stated that the calls ranged from domestics with stabbings, shootings, one shovel assault to a drive by shootings with automatic weapons resulting in seven dead and thirteen in the hospital with serious wounds. The streets were still on fire with people demonstrating the beast within.

The power shift, which overlapped the afternoon and midnight shifts, had all the squad cars tied up on violent calls. The midnight crew needed to get to their cars and active ASAP. Roll call broke off immediately. Frank and Jerry went to the squad car assigned to them by Lopez. Frank got into the driver's seat, calling himself the "Squad Commander" while Jerry picked up the joke calling himself the "Communications Director", meaning that he was riding shotgun and would be the one who would answer all the radio calls. Jerry picked up the microphone and checked-in, "Squad 711 is in service." The dispatcher answered and sent them on a call. "Squad 711, in service. Go to 438 W. Main on a domestic with shots fired." Jerry answered, "Squad 711, 104 from HQ." Frank drove the Ford out of the parking lot in the rear of the headquarters building where the city jail was located on the third floor. They drove to 438 West Main, as directed, and located the house on the north side of Main Street and noticed right away that they really didn't need the street address as the whole neighborhood seemed to be on the front lawn. The lights were on inside the home and silhouetted figures doing a lot of movement indicated the process of a domestic fight was still in full force. It amazed both officers that there were so many people within the immediate vicinity especially since there was a report of shots being fired. When they exited the squad two shots rang out from the home. The crowd on the lawn cheered and closed the distance between them and the danger within the home. Jerry grabbed the shotgun. They both ran to the porch, positioning themselves on either side of the front door. Frank yelled, "Police. Put down your weapons and come out on the porch. Do it now!" With their weapons at ready both officers waited by the door anticipating and praying for a peaceful ending to this violent situation.

Instead the door flung open with two guns firing simultaneously, reminiscent of an old cowboy movie. A large black male, emerged from the house yelling at the top of his voice and called out to the crowd, "I'll kill ya'. I'll kill every one of ya'. I'll kill ya'. I'll kill ya'." With that announcement he started shooting randomly into the crowd. Two people, a man and a woman, dropped to the ground, withering in pain, screaming out loudly. This again excited the crowd and encouragement from them caused another volley of bullets to escape from the man's automatic handguns. Again people dropped from the audience on the front lawn. Three men dropped dead on the spot and two women fell critically wounded. Jerry opened up with the 12 ga. Winchester pump shotgun that he had secured from the squad car. The full force of the double 00 buck shotgun blast from three shells, jacked into the gun, did more than a little damage to the large black man who was picked up from the grassy lawn and hurled towards the excited group of spectators, adding to their obvious enjoyment of the night's festivities. When he hit the ground, with a large gaping wound visible in the trunk of his body, he ceased to move but the crowd wouldn't allow him to die.

They wanted more shooting and blood spurting from the open puncture wounds, not only on him but the individuals he had shot. Half of the crowd, the ones still on their feet, rushed to him and tried lifting him up. A couple of the men attempted to put the guns back into his limp hands. The people, trying to revive the dead man, received encouraging words from the rest of the crowd.

When they were unable to bring the man back to life, the two men who were trying to put the guns in his hands took control of the weapons themselves. Both men turned towards the police officers and opened fire. Frank and partner Jerry responded by returning fire; however because of their training at the range all those years, hit their targets, whereas the two men from the crowded lawn missed completely. The crowd again erupted with the pleasure of seeing someone die. Not knowing what would happen next, they kept their weapons trained on the group of people in front of them on the lawn. With the absence of blood, screams of pain and death, the crowd slowly dispersed into the streets and the nearby yards.

The whole thing happened so fast that neither officer had the opportunity to call for back up, so with the shooting over, they not only contacted Sgt. Lopez but started searching the house which had been the origin of the violence. Lopez informed them, as they searched the house, that he wouldn't be able to respond soon. He too was involved with another shooting call and was in the process of assisting the officers on that call. Their attempt to contact Lt. Ward was equally frustrating. The house's interior was a shock to both officers even though they had a combined 20 years on the job and thought that they had seen everything that there was to see. The living room was the scene of a brutal triple murder of children. All three had been hacked up using a machete that was left on the bloody floor. Frank couldn't handle this scene or the killing outside and had to rush into the kitchen for the purpose of emptying his stomach's contents. Even in the kitchen there were remains of the evil that had filled the house.

There was the still body of a black woman, who had been shot several times at close range, resting against the legs of the kitchen table. Her face held the death mask of the horror she had seen just before she died. When Frank had finished at the sink he turned back from where he had come and his eyes filled with the gruesome sight of the dead woman whose eyes, even in death, caught his stare and returned the same. The previous sight of the children, the smell of the house's interior and now the woman's blank stare repulsed Frank enough to turn him again to the sink.

Jerry was stuck in the living room where the sight of the bodies of the small children held him captive. Jerry couldn't move. He was transfixed within the evidence of the most extreme evil he had ever experienced in his life. It wasn't the sight of the dead that consumed him so completely but the knowledge that true and pure evil had been where he now stood. His mind numbed and his extremities became useless.

When Frank returned to Jerry, the paralyzing trance broke and he was able to remove himself from the horror long enough to start performing his duties as a cop.

Neither officer talked to each other but started controlling the scene so that the investigation could begin by the crime lab. The two cops wouldn't actually do the processing themselves but Frank initiated the process of control by starting up the stairs to get a couple of sheets to cover the bodies. The upstairs was as shocking to him as was the lower floor. Everything was clean, pristine and in place. There was absolutely no indication there of the carnage that had taken place below. It reminded him of the effects of a tornado. He saw what a tornado could do once a couple of years ago. He observed that it left debris on one side of a fence and a doll carriage with the doll still in it untouched on the other side, just a couple of feet away. He saw half a house. One side missing and the other side still in place with the bed made as if ready to be occupied for a night's rest even though there was a wall missing in the bedroom. Frank went into the bathroom closet and retrieved all the sheets that were there and three large bath towels to cover the children. As he started down the stairs with the sheets and towels the smell of death hit him again. He realized for the first time that the smell had been missing from upstairs. There was a huge difference between the two floors and that difference disturbed him even more than the gruesome sight that had touched him so negatively when he first entered the house.

He found himself breathing through his mouth rather than through his nose as he covered the three kids with the towels. The smell was overpowering and he was getting sick again. To squelch the feelings of nausea he started the mouth breathing. Jerry, mouth breathing as well, was taking pictures with the digital camera he had retrieved from the trunk of the squad car. Frank waited until Jerry had taken all the pictures of the bodies before covering them. There were so many pictures to take that Jerry had trouble keeping a log of the ones already done and had to ask his partner to help him make out the picture log. This was the first time either man spoke since they came into this scene of horrors.

Soon the lab truck arrived with the civilian lab technicians to process the scene completely. They had been going from one murder scene to the next without a break. They were exhausted but went to work immediately. It was unusual for the crew to go directly to the scene without exchanging pleasantries, of sort, with the cops at the scene. It was their way of bonding with the members of the force. It was a very few individuals who were let into the "brotherhood of the blue" and the lab crew were allowed that honor. They didn't stop or even acknowledge Frank and Jerry as they started gathering evidence. The last body to be covered was the black man who had been almost blown in half by the shotgun blast. The crowd that was on the front lawn had all gone away leaving only its former participants dead where they had once stood to witness the devil's work first hand. The front lawn also smelled of the evil stench left by the dead. Frank wondered how long the smell would linger not only in the house but on the lawn as well.

Frank put the keys into the ignition and Jerry picked up the microphone inside the squad car to put them back into service. They were ready to leave the call after turning the crime scene over to the lab crew. The twelve dead people they left behind who would haunt the two men for the rest of their lives but the night was still young and there were more calls yet to be answered. They had been on the streets two hours now and the reports concerning the call were still in need of being written. Normally the two officers would have kept their squad out of service until the reports were complete but this was an unusual night and they knew they needed to be in service as soon as possible.

Jerry told the dispatcher they were back in service and asked for a complaint number (CN) to be used on the reports when they were to be written later that night. The dispatcher gave them the CN and the next call at the same time. The night was a busy one and they were back into it again. "Squad 711. Go to the corner of Market and 35th Street on a violent crowd gathering with shots fired." " Squad 711 received." answered Jerry. He looked at Frank who gave him one of those rolled eye looks that is always received in the same manner it was sent. Jerry pulled the shotgun from its locked rest, where he had just placed it and dug out three double 00 buck shotgun shells from the compartment located between them in the front seat. He loaded the 12 gauge and kept it close to him in preparation for their next call.

What they saw when they arrived was almost identical to their first call in that there were too many people milling around where shots had been fired. No one fled for their own safety into hiding places. There were two groups of people standing in the middle of the intersection of Market & 35th divided by only a couple yards of pavement beneath their feet. The two groups were also separated by ethnicity even wider than the gap dividing them physically. One group consisted completely of male Hispanics while the other was the tough, Caucasian, biker type; mostly males but a few "biker babes" completed the crowd. The fire department's paramedic squads had responded prior to 711's arrival. There were four paramedics administering to someone lying on the cement sidewalk in front of the salon named "Billy's Biker Bar". Bikers were huddled around the paramedics. The bar had been shut down by the power shift (8pm to 4am) around 11:00pm because of fights inside the establishment. The bikers spilled out onto the street and some continued the aggression that caused the bar's closing. The Hispanics came from a house party just down Market Street, two houses. They came into the street when one of the bikers had said something derogatory to a female guest arriving for the party. She had gone in the house to tell her story at which time all the male populations at the party were eager to respond. The person on the sidewalk was not moving even though the firemen were working hard to revive him. The Hispanic group was yelling insults at the bikers but at this point the bikers seemed to be deaf to the constant badgering. They were more intent on the outcome of the firemen's efforts.

Frank walked over to where he could get some information from the paramedics who were working on the fallen man. One of the paramedics stood up and told Frank, in a tone that he should have whispered, but instead came out clearly audible to the bikers in close proximity, that the man was dead. The bikers repeated the message throughout the group until there was no question left unanswered about "Fred's condition". Fred was dead and the bikers wanted revenge. It became apparent to Frank and Jerry immediately that the revenge would be aimed at the Hispanic crowd.

The bikers pulled handguns from everywhere on their person and bullets flew into the group standing only a few feet from them. The Hispanics drew their weapons and returned fire into the bikers. Frank and Jerry joined the paramedics who left the lifeless body of "Fred" on the sidewalk and fled to a safety zone on the other side of the ambulance.

When the shots stopped the two officers came out from behind the safety of the white vehicle to see not one person standing in the street. There was over thirty dead or dying human beings to add to the total number of causalities from this night's list of tragedies. They had their weapon at ready, Frank with his Glock and Jerry with the shotgun. There was no one to cover or to declare the order: "Cease firing and drop your weapons".

A couple of bikers and a few more Hispanics withering in pain and close to death were the only ones moving on the street. There was no threat to either officer and they lowered their artillery.

This was the second event this evening, where the two officers had witnessed the mass destruction of life. They looked at each other's eyes searching for an explanation but not even a guess could be offered by either. The streets were all wrong. The senseless loss of so many lives defined logic. In the ten years of police work neither officer had experienced the carnage, the unreasonable sights they had witnessed this night.

The paramedics had been on duty for the third day now, on a shift that went from three days on to four days off. They had gone from call to call continuously, in the presence of the evil that had filled the streets. They had all gone numb at the sights of the horror and the experience of extreme wickedness over the last few days. This evening was the worst of the three days and evenings they had spent answering the dreaded calls. The senseless bloodshed clouded their minds until they were only working on the bodies of people and not the people. The humanity disappeared to them and they simply administered to the warm bodies of the dying. The night had taken its victims and some of those victims were the paramedics.

With the paramedics trying to determine who was alive and who was dead in the streets near the bar, Frank and Jerry left the crime scene to the firefighters/ paramedics. They again entered the security of their squad car. Both men sat in silence for what seemed like an eternity but was actually only about five minutes.

Frank again started the Ford while Jerry placed the shotgun back in the rest and pushed the lock close. Jerry didn't want to pick up the microphone and announce that they were done at a call. A call in which all the people on the street were dead or dying. He didn't want to say that squad 711 was ready to answer the next horrible assignment. Nevertheless he did pick it up and check into service. The dispatchers told them to proceed to a down town address where there numerous reports of looting going on at many of the businesses. Frank put the car into gear and rolled forward with no intent of turning on the blue lights that sat over their heads on the roof of the squad. He wasn't about to drive over the speed limit. Frank was in no hurry to get to the next scene of an unwanted adrenalin rush. It was often said that all cops are drug addicts and their choice of drugs was adrenalin. This evening these two drug addicts wanted nothing to with their drug of choice. They were west of the down town area, a trip on a normal night would have taken 15 minutes with the blue light special in full form. However this was not a normal night by anyone's imagination and the break neck speed of less than 35 miles an hour was not the only thing that slowed the squad's response time.

It was approaching 3:00am and the streets should have been empting of the night owl inhabitants. This was not the case. People were coming out of the woodwork by the numbers. There were fights, too many to count, on almost every street corner as they passed. The violence had increased instead of decreasing with the late night or early morning hours depending on your point of view. On a normal night the fights would have stopped the squad and arrests would have been initiated. Not tonight.

The downtown part of the city sat in a shallow valley and located dead center to all its boundaries. As the squad car topped the hill called Ramsey Hill the two officers saw a bright glow emanating from the very center of down town. There was no question that the glow was the product of a large fire or many small ones. Maybe the looters had set fire to the store fronts as they pillaged the items from the broken windows. The closer they got to the center of down town the more came into view and it wasn't pretty. The streets were alive with insanity. There was no resemblance of anything normal and the deeper to the middle they drove the more it became apparent the whole downtown area was deep in the clutches of extreme evil. The former humans were breaking everything they could get their hands on which included: The front windows to the shops, the contents of the display windows, the park benches located on the sidewalks, all the trash containers placed by the corners of the streets and directional signs put in place by the highway departments. All the items had been turned into weapons used to smash heads, cut large gashes into bodies, disemboweling the unlucky, break the back of a passerby and kill all who were near.

It was too much for Frank to endure. He stopped the car and just sat in the driver's seat not knowing what to do next. There was so much crime going on all around them and to pick a starting point, used for the purpose of deterring the rioting crowd, was impossible. Without communicating to Jerry of his intent, Frank put the squad into low and squealed the tires making the vehicle jumped into the mass of what was one time, human beings. The bodies of men and women flew into the air and fell behind the car as Frank continued striking the people in the street in front of them, with the vehicular weapon. Jerry's eyes widened as he took in what was happening yet couldn't believe what he was seeing. "What the hell are you doing? Stop! Stop it right now! Frank Stop!"

Frank didn't stop and the parade of beings didn't stop either. There seemed to be no end to the number of people that remained unmoving in front of the vehicle that was killing almost all of them. People were not moving out of the way. They didn't appear to care if they were run over by the speeding squad that was now picking up more speed as it crushed people or flung them into the air. Jerry was screaming his pleads to Frank who was listening with deaf ears. "Frank! Stop. Please stop!" Jerry had tears coming to his eyes as he pulled his service Glock automatic 9 millimeter from its holster. "Oh God, Frank. Please stop. Stop right now. Please." Tears were flowing as he pleaded with his partner. Jerry aimed his automatic at Frank's head and now ordered him, "Stop killing these people." Frank didn't acknowledge Jerry's voice, his fears, his pleads, his tears. He didn't acknowledge the hand gun aimed at his right temple. Frank didn't indicate that he knew what he was doing or what was coming because of his actions. Frank kept driving or better said, aiming at the crowd of people who still filled the street and whom he was destroying with the Ford leaving a trail of bloody bodies behind.

Jerry didn't hear the report of his weapon but jumped a little when it went off. Blood from his partner's head filled the interior of the car. There was a hole about two inches in diameter in the center of the driver's window. Frank's body leaned to the left and grotesquely slumped between the door and the steering wheel.

Jerry now crying hysterically called out, "Oh my God. Where are you, Lord? Why is this happening? My Lord. My God. Where are YOU?" Jerry placed the barrel of the Glock in his mouth and pulled the trigger.

CHAPTER SEVEN

RIOTS

The news media finally started reporting some of the more violent episodes of rioting throughout the country's larger cities. The radio and television stations were first, followed by the newspapers. Only the local coverage actively followed the stories though, not one of the national stations picked up on the small riots even though people had lost their lives at every scene. The media was afraid to report the activity because no one could come up with a cause, which left the stories unfinished and even questionable to the public. Reporters balked when told to cover the stories. They didn't want the public to see them as unreliable or just plain stupid. Yet one by one the larger city's media sources had to start covering the riots. It was the Midwest cities that responded to the need for coverage by both the radio and television stations initially. Kansas City, Oklahoma City, Omaha, Des Moines and Little Rock all responded to the public's constant pressure to report stories of the rioting. The public wanted to know what happened and more importantly why it happened.

At first, reporters told the listeners, "The riots broke out for no apparent reason....", or "A violet response to an undetermined cause...." Not one reporter ventured a guess for fear of being wrong and finding a law suit parked on their door step.

Then one young, lady reporter named Virginia Billows in Omaha, told her listening audience that the riots had been caused by the public outcry about the injustice within the government of the United States. It was her liberal tendencies and prejudices about a conservative occupied presidency and the congress that brought her to make that statement in public without proof. Other news agencies picked up on her comment and pretty soon it became gospel to all who were reporting the riots.

All the riots started in the evening and lasted into the morning hours of the next day. It didn't matter what the weather was like, the riots would take place in the rain, in the snow, in the sleet or in good weather. The rioters would one second be strolling down the sidewalk talking to each other and the next second clubbing each other over the head with whatever was handy to do damage to humans and to property alike. When the police responded to the calls they would find themselves in a land of zombies. Unlike any previous situations akin of rioting, for which they had been trained, there was no leader or apparent cause that lit up the streets with senseless violence. This led them into unchartered waters of human brutality for which they were unprepared. The individual police officer had everything to do not to join in the hostility. The temptation to just start responding with equal or more than equal senseless aggression was difficult to suppress. They were ill prepared to deal with the eruptions and because of that, the riots went into the final phases on regularity which mean there were deaths that ended the violence.

Each violent eruption started the same way and ended the same way. That was the only thing about the riots they were able to identify as similar and tried to learn how to cope with the situations, from that information. It didn't really help.

Then a very strange happening occurred at most of the scenes after the riots: protesters showed up in force. People with signs marching in unison in the debris of the aftermath brought on by the carnage. Young people mostly, with a sprinkle of middle aged blue collared workers; the majority of both groups were men. There it was: an unusual peaceful assembly on the morning after a horrible night. The obvious contrast was not lost on the media. After the first few gatherings were reported to the media by concerned citizens, the television stations started sending their remote units back to the scene of the riots the following morning to cover the protestors. The sign carrying protesters showed up anywhere from 9:00am to 11:30am. It was apparent that the protests were not organized. Once the local media started reporting the gatherings other cities recognized they too were having the unorganized protests following the riots. There was no chanting, no loud voices shouting together one particular slogan or any indication of a point being announced by the protesters. The only indication that the people who were gathered for the peaceful assemblies were there to protest was the signs they carried.

The signs were not professionally rendered but instead each was handmade. The poster board came only in white, no colors were carried. The printing, done mostly with a felt ink pen, was provided in only three different colors: red, green and blue. There were no pictures, no drawings or caricatures on the posters, only the written words. The words could never be interpreted as threats or warnings but as notification of what should be a concern to all who could read them. It was apparent to the onlookers; Virginia Billows of Omaha had spoken words that had left an impression.

The posters contained thoughts like: The Government is the People, All people have Rights, Our Government is Different…What has Changed? Violence is not the Answer to any Question, Why are Riots? We should NEVER accept the loss of life, and The Answer **IS** LIFE **NOT** DEATH!

The riots and the following gathering of people with posters continued for months across the Midwest in different cities, never repeated in the same place twice. Death always followed the riots and the posters always followed the deaths. Never were the posters printed in an offensive manner, never were the protesters vocal or abusive and never were they the same people from the other protests. The individuals who showed up were mixed from the same previous batter of mostly young men and blue collar workers. The city police departments continued to be perplexed and unable to do anything to curtail the violence or stop the loss of life.

The departments communicated with each other only after they had experienced a riot but the riots never happened in the same place, so the police in the next town or city had no information to help them. It was a vicious circle that remained unbroken and the death count grew.

Thirty-six cities had been affected by the cruelty of the riots and the loss of human life, when Springfield, Missouri erupted at 10:39pm into a war theatre of destruction and mayhem. Springfield became number thirty-seven. Business' show windows broke out when heavy items from the street were thrown through them. Fires started, in the windows, after the televisions, radios, CD players, clothing or furniture were removed or destroyed. Vehicles with license plates, originating from all over the country, were crashed into walls and window fronts of the buildings downtown. Zombie like people ran down the streets and sidewalks with no intent of getting anywhere in particular, just running with blank faces.

Springfield, Missouri's pride and number one attraction The Bass Pro Shop got hit about 2:00am with a storm of wild eyed, freaks of humanity. Large pontoon boats, bass fishing rigs, smaller pleasure boats and john boats were turned over one on the other, with unreal strength from inhuman people. The front doors were bludgeoned with old discarded telephone poles until the huge doors finally crumbled. The collection of taxidermy, antique fishing reels and lures all succumbed to the onrush of mad men and women intent on destruction. The glass aquarium containing hundreds of native fish exploded when the front was penetrated by a 12 ga. shotgun blast, followed by three or four 30.06 shots, fired from one of the store's many rifles. Other shots rang out through the huge building and people dropped where they stood, victims of more senseless killing. The weaponry was simply removed from where it was kept, loaded with the available ammunition and shot into the crowd. Screams of pain followed by animalistic hollering intended to encourage more murder filled the giant sporting goods store.

Jeff Bloom drove to his night job of stocking shelves at the famous Bass Pro Shop across town. He left a little early because he wanted to stop at the gas station to pick up some cigarettes. He got almost to West Sunshine off of Glendale Ave. when his car was stopped by a wild crowd of angry people forming a human blockade in the middle of the street. He got out of his car to ask what was happening and immediately lost all sense of reality. He became furious over nothing.

His anger was directed at everything and nothing at the same time. He could not relate to what happened all around him. He wanted to, no he needed to destroy something or someone and it didn't matter who or what. He was a large man at 269 lbs., standing 6 foot 3 inches with no fat around his waist. Not yet 35, having matured early or so it seemed, because his hair had turned white at the age of 28. Jeff was someone a person could depend upon for whatever was needed. He could be trusted with any project, any secret or any need you might have. What he had turned into was exactly the opposite of who he was or ever had been. Jeff was a predator looking for a kill.

He abandoned his car, still running, in the middle of the street and joined the rioters as they traveled west, destroying everything in their pathway. No one had been murdered yet, though it wasn't without possibility the more the group progressed and added to its number. Jeff entered his place of employment, acting like anything but a representative of the company that paid his wages. He picked up some of the more easily attained fish mounts and threw them into the air. His area of expertise is where he went to next, not so much out of habit, but more of blind wandering.

It lasted no more than a fraction of a second when his mind cleared and he looked around the store taking in the tragic scene unfolding in front of him. He was in the area where the fly fishing rods, reels, floating line were placed on display. This was his area. From where the fly fishing equipment was displayed, he could also see the guns. The crowd of terror moved in that direction reaping havoc on the way. Sporting equipment was thrown, torn, broken and mangled as the group destroyed Bass Pro Shop from the inside. As fast as he had returned to his normal mind, his mind rushed back to the zombie like state that he had assumed when his car stopped.

Jeff, the mad man, rushed to the rear of the store where the extremely large aquarium was located. In his normal state, Jeff would take all his night breaks in front of the fish and enjoy watching their leisurely life in the water. Sometimes, on his day off, he would even come by the store just to sit and watch the frogman, whose name was Tim Jones, get into the tank and feed the fish by hand. This was Jeff's favorite place in the huge sporting goods store, but not tonight. This night found him again in front of the fish tank, without knowledge of how he arrived there and without concern.

He jumped when the first shot rang out. The noise, so loud, hurt his ears and made him even angrier. The report came from the Remington pump shotgun taken from where it had been displayed and loaded on the spot with 12 ga. number 2 shot. The first shot fractured the glass but it held the weight of the water back. The second shot, not from the shot gun, did the trick. A 30.06 cal. Winchester bolt action rifle had also been taken down, loaded and fired by another person standing on the Jeff's right. Again the loud report made

Jeff's ears hurt. He grabbed at the sides of his head and tried to cover his ears.

He turned toward the source of the loud, painful explosion and saw the man with the rifle. He growled. The growl came from a primeval center of the animal within Jeff and his intent was clear to anyone in their right mind but there were none around. Showing his teeth through curled lips he advanced in the direction of the man holding the weapon. In real life Jeff's movement would have been seen and the rifle would have been pointed at Jeff in time to stop his advance. This was not a normal night and what happened next was not normal either. Jeff advanced slowly, threatening with primitive sounds and animalistic facial features. The man holding the Winchester looking directly at Jeff and didn't recognize the life threatening event that unfolded in front of him.

Jeff grabbed the rifle in the man's hands and threw him sideways using the weapon to toss him aside. The man, who was smaller than his attacker, lost his balance and then his grip on the rifle. He fell on his back, staring up at the ceiling blankly, not understanding what had just happened to him or comprehending what came next. Jeff used the weapon he had just ceased and fired one shot into the man's chest. Jeff had committed his first murder of the night. More were to come.

Jeff, with no remorse, went from the scene of the broken aquarium, the floor wet and full of flopping, bass, bluegill, channel cat, crappie, carp and blood from the newly murdered man, to join the group as they proceeded to the mountain of mounts. Deer, caribou, bear, wolves and mountain sheep mounts were torn from their stands and tossed around and down the fake mountain. Heads of the mounted specimens were ripped off the bodies and discarded for no purpose other than destruction.

Jeff saw a younger man pull a re-curve bow off the shelf and open a box of field tipped arrows. Soon the young man was shooting into the crowd one arrow after another. Some people dropped dead while others screamed out in pain as the arrows hit spots that were not fatal. There were twelve arrows in the box and the man continued shooting until the arrows were all used, then threw the bow aside and disappeared into the crowd.

At 4:27am the riot stopped just like it had started. There was no reason it began and no reason it ended. Jeff, no longer a madman, looked around at the inside of his place of employment and recognized nothing. The store had been completely destroyed. More disturbing to Jeff, were the bodies he discovered in the rubble as he tried to make his way out of the building. He couldn't remember how he got there nor the carnage of which he had been a part. He had become a murderer and had no recollection of the act, so he had no remorse. There were cops all over the parking lot and at the entrances to the store when he finally found his way out. Not one police officer had ventured into the rampage in the store while it was in full force. The store had become a war zone and with no training and no desire to take on a larger force full of insanity, the department's orders were to control the perimeter until it stopped. Arrests were made as soon as the rioters emerged from the building, but there were too many rioters and too few police officers to accomplish much more that a feeble attempt. None of the newly arrested members of the groups put up any resistance; in fact they were perplexed at the whole scene surrounding them. Most of the participants simply walked past the police, into the early morning darkness and went home. They were tired. Jeff was exhausted. He walked into the darkness like so many others. A murderer walked free.

The Springfield media showed up at 5:00am at the spot where Bass Pro Shop had stood. The building was intact, but that was all that resembled what had been there before. The most obvious change outside was all the boats, big and small. It looked like a tornado had blown through and left its mess behind. The cameras were immediately aimed in that direction. All the television reporters faced the cameras with the water craft debris in the background. The first of the descriptions reported by the radio was the wreckage of the boats. The site was impressive to anyone who saw the damage but they hadn't gone inside yet.

The Chief of Police, Scott Flowers, availed himself to the news reporters but wouldn't let anyone inside. It was a crime scene still being processed. When the police went in, shortly after the arrests were effected, they had discovered thirty dead bodies. Some people had been shot by guns, others had been punctured with arrows and a few had been just run over by the mass of humanity gone crazy. The city coroner had been contacted and taken the first of the bodies back to the morgue. There were too many to remove from the scene at once. The individuals killed had been both men and women. The second transportation of the dead took less time. Some of the pictures of the city transporting the bodies were placed on the front page alongside pictures of the boat devastation. The radio and television reported that the "looters' had killed numerous people at the scene of the Bass Pro Shop riot.

Citizens waited outside the morgue hoping that they wouldn't find their missing relatives in the cold storage. Many people from the night before had not returned home and had not been arrested at the shop. They were just missing. Springfield always had a lot of tourists visiting most of the time of the year, so the streets were always busy. This morning it wasn't visitors, it was local people out in their vehicles looking for missing family members. Some of the missing people were located sitting on the curbs of the street. Others were located wandering aimlessly in the alleyways down town. Some were found in the parks, sitting on benches. All of the recovered family members were confused and despondent.

Jeff walked down the middle of the street in a direction that would accomplish nothing. He wasn't heading home or any other destination that would have been chosen by him any other morning. Something was wrong, very wrong, but Jeff had no idea what it might be. The street, where he had accidently found himself, lacked the common street lights most other streets in Springfield had and it was still pre-dawn.

It was a 2006 Black Ford pickup 150 with two male passengers of high school age. Neither of the boys had been involved with the night's activities at the Bass Pro Shop. They had snuck out of their houses to go on a pre-planned drunk, trying to be something other than who they were. It was very unusual for these two boys because they had always been dependable, straight "A" students, but were sick and tired of being "that kind of kid".

They started the venture about 2:30am, when they were sure their parents were sound asleep. By 5:15am they were "tuned to the gills" and trying to find their way home.

Franklin Smith drove and Alexander Bodkin snoozed, leaning on the window of the passenger's side. Frankie, if he had to, would have registered a .14 B.A.C. on a breathalyzer, more than twice the legal limit for Missouri. The black Ford traveled from one lane to the other at a speed in access of 50mph. Frankie was talking incessantly, about nothing, in an effort to stay awake, even though his eyelids were intent on closing. He claimed to the police officer, later that morning, that he never saw the man walking down the middle of the street, before hitting him.

Jeff died in the middle of the street, broken back and fractured skull. Jeff didn't suffer. He never knew what hit him. Frankie was placed under arrest for vehicular homicide and DUI, taken to headquarters to run a breathalyzer and Alexander was taken into custody for minor consumption. Another death had occurred that was indirectly related to the strange happenings from the night before. Springfield, Missouri was the unwilling recipient of the latest unexplained change in the nature of man. Springfield became another city in the Midwest that saw the horror of the senseless destruction and instant insanity of its population gone over the edge of normal behavior, into the depth of inhuman madness.

The first of the protesters, a young man named Douglas Thomas, showed up where Bass Pro had been a thriving business the day before. He wore blue jeans and a gray sweat shirt. The sign he carried had been hand written, using a black felt pen on white poster board. The sign read: "Humanity Should Never Lose Its Human Side". It was 10:45am when the second protester came to the scene, followed shortly by six others. By 11:30 am there were seventeen people all carrying signs made of poster board tacked to long pieces of 1"X 2" pine. One of the poster boards, written in green on white, read: "We Have Kicked God Out Of Our Lives. Now What?"

It was the first mention of God at any of the protests. Finally someone had hit on the root cause of the riots that caused destruction of property and loss of life. This poster at the Bass Pro Shop was the first of its kind. Many more were to come that would identify what was wrong in the country, before it would end.

CHAPTER EIGHT

THE DREAMS

Fr. Tom Kennedy was the first one to experience the bad dreams. He couldn't describe them as nightmares because they didn't have anything he could relate to from his past that he would have described as nightmares. They weren't frightening, yet he would wake in the middle of the night in a cold sweat. He thought that maybe the recent type of confessions he was hearing had caused the bad dreams. The first of the strange confessions started with a young boy who had not so much confessed his sins to the priest but seemed to be bragging about his evil doings. It was then followed by the same incredible string of sinners who didn't appear to have any need to confess, but instead, tell their stories of horror. He had even considered not granting absolution, but couldn't nail down from what he was hearing, that which would allow him to retain forgiveness. It was just a feeling that he was getting from each person who would enter the confessional. They weren't there for the purpose of the sacrament, nothing substantial for him to react to at all.

Tom had a spiritual advisor, as do almost all priests, named Fr. Terry Fenwick who was the pastor of the nearest church to where Tom was assigned. It was a short drive every other Friday afternoon to Christ the King Catholic Church's rectory where Terry would listen to Tom's life stories and advise him not only in his spiritual but his secular life as well. Terry was a good friend as well. On this particular Friday, Tom shared his bad dreams and was amazed to learn that Terry had been experiencing something similar. So the two priests compared dreams rather than the usual time spent in their different roles, one as a confessor and the other as a guide through a particular religious life.

Tom told Terry that the dream was like nothing he had ever had before. It was dark! That was the only way he could explain to Terry what it was like. It was completely black. There was no light in the presence of what he saw. The completed absence of light was overwhelming. He could feel himself begin to panic and couldn't stop the feeling of extreme helplessness. All his attempts to find a pathway, a window, a door or even a wall were left unsuccessful. He woke in a wet bed, wet from the sweat that poured from all parts of his body. The panic of his dream woke with him and accompanied him for most of the morning. It was a feeling that he couldn't depart from, or his mind wouldn't let him get rid of, no matter how much he prayed or tried to change his thoughts. Each time he had the dream the same thing happened: he couldn't get away from it. The more times he had the dream the longer the feeling stayed with him. He found himself at the foot of the altar in the church, praying for forgiveness and not knowing why. He felt that somehow the guilt he was also feeling may have caused such distress in his sleep and waking hours.

Terry explained to Tom that he, too, had been experiencing extremely troubled sleep. He had tried to stay awake for fear of having the dream come back again. He was becoming sleep deprived and found his mind wandering back to the feeling that woke him too many times in the last few weeks. Terry described the dreams differently than Tom. He explained that the dream presented him with a complete emptiness, so complete that he couldn't find the worth of anything that he valued in his life. The emptiness sucked his soul dry. It filled his very being with nothing. It was a vacuum that consumed his heart. Terry felt a deep sorrow that pushed him to uncontrollable sobbing.

He would wake from the dream with a wet pillow, soaked with the salty liquid that poured from his eyes. The lack of worth, the emptiness, the vacuum accompanied him as the darkness had followed Tom into his day.

The similarities, for the priests, were difficult to find other than the overwhelming feelings that consumed their waking hours since the bad dreams had started. The darkness and the emptiness were explained as "not the same" by both men. They seem hard pressed to let go of the fact that the dreams were actually very similar in nature. Neither had ever had such a dream, unable to compare them to a nightmare, there was really no substance to the dreams, just feelings totally overwhelming to both of them. Yet they refused to allow those comparisons to be agreed upon. They didn't want their dreams to be the same. They wanted to possess their own and not share the similarities. It was said that dreams are personal; to these two men the dreams were more than personal. The dreams were precious belongings, guarded as a pirate guards his ill-gotten booty.

Tom was not satisfied with the visit that day. He left with no directions from his advisor. No passages in the bible to help him meditate or direct him to a spiritual solution. No shared advice to reflect upon that would offer help with his sleep struggles. No feeling of relief, like those other Fridays of the last four years. Tom was disheartened and confused. He tried to pray on the short drive back to his parish. The words didn't come easy in his prayer. All he could say to God was that he was sorry, and Tom didn't know what he should be sorry about.

Terry was equally dissatisfied with the visit. He didn't know why he didn't have the ability to help his friend with the same trouble he was having himself. He had always felt like he had accomplished what he had been taught to do in the seminary and then at some special classes he took at the nearby college, when Tom left for the day. This day nothing had been accomplished and was as empty a feeling as his dreams. He went to his church and knelt for prayer in one of the back pews. The words came hard to Terry as he tried to put into some understandable form of communication, something that would satisfy his need to talk to God. All he could remember was an act of contrition that had been taught to him by one of the nuns he had as a teacher in grade school. He didn't know why that prayer was the only one he could come up with, or why he felt the need for forgiveness.

It was Saturday afternoon and Tom was beginning to perspire already. The time for confessions was soon approaching and his love of the sacrament had dwindled over the past few weeks. He didn't want to go over to the church, sit in the small chamber of the confessional and listen to parishioners brag about their sins and corrupt life. Small little steps, one after the other and Tom found himself walking through the backdoor of the church making his way to the right side of the big building where the confessional was located. He groaned a big sigh and opened the door to the middle chamber where he would sit until no more people came in.

Joanne, a parishioner, was of a nondescript personality to Tom or any of the 500 other regulars who attended church. She was not married and probably never will be. Her clothes were out-of-date and complemented her out-of- date hairdo, completing her persona to the public. She would have been type cast as a librarian in any "B" class movie. That would have been funny if she wasn't working in the public library going on her 15th year. Joanne attended Mass every Sunday and went to confession as often as she thought she needed to, but she very seldom really needed to. Today was different.

She was having bad dreams for about three weeks. Her night's sleep had gone from 7 to 8 hours nightly to less than two. She would wake up numerous times at first and as the nights dragged on, she would awaken so many times that the two hours per night was now the norm. Joanne had always been a person who needed her sleep. She had a sister named Brenda who was the night owl and in her youth, a party girl who relished the night life and didn't need her sleep to recover. Joanne was definitely not her sister. The lack of sleep was affecting her health. The headaches and constant nausea forced vomiting so she wasn't able to keep anything on her stomach. The more she vomited the worst her health became.

Her strength was slowly leaving her and a sickness was beginning to creep in. It was the dreams that kept her from her much needed slumber. The dreams were vacant of any substance; there was only a feeling when she woke in the middle of the night. The feeling was fear. She couldn't explain the reason for the fear to anybody, though she tried. She attempted to tell Brenda and some of her close friends, but no one was really interested in listening to her problems.

The dreams that kept her awake didn't give her a reason to be afraid, yet when she sat up straight in bed, the fear was overwhelming though she had no memory of the dream. How does one explain to another that there was no reason she could remember to cause it but the fear was real. It was this lack of ability to describe, to convince, to share her horror that pushed her to the one place in her life where she always felt relief; the confessional.

Using the holy water font she crossed herself, genuflected and entered a pew fairly close to the three small cubicles used by the faithful and their priests.

She bowed her head in prayer and felt the nausea, causing her a dizziness that forced her into what the Catholics called a "three point landing". With her knees on the kneeler, her head still bowed and resting on her arms on the pew in front of her, she sat in the seat completing the "three point landing". The dizziness didn't dissipate and the nausea pushed the issue. She had to actually sit in the seat before fainting would occur. The confessional's right side was exited by a large lady who went directly to the collection of candles located at the feet of the statue of the Virgin Mary. The woman lit one of the smaller candles and knelt down, bowed head and Joanne assumed she prayed her penance.

No one was standing in a line so Joanne sucked up her feeling of the fainting dizziness, stood up, and made her way to the chamber that had been vacated by the lady kneeling in front of the candles and the statue of Mary. She entered the semi-darkened cubical. She heard the small screened window slide sideways. The opaque curtain that separated the priest from the faithful kneeling on the other side of the window, did not allow either to see the other. "Bless me Father, for I have sinned. My last confession........" The words came easily. She had spoken them since she was a little girl just prior to receiving her First Communion. The sins confessed then were extremely different from the ones for which she begged forgiveness later in life. A priest friend of hers once told her that hearing the confessions of children and nuns was like being beaten to death with a feather. Today, this Saturday was not about confessing sins but more of a deep need to obtain an understanding from somebody she respected and possibly relief.

She continued but not with the words she had learned as a child from some nun, "Father this is not about my last confession or even this one. I need to talk to someone about not sleeping." Fr. Tom didn't understand what he heard, "About sleeping with some one?" He inquired. He was too used to hearing the continuous barrage of sinful bragging.

Joanne responded, "No Father, I need to tell someone about these damn dreams. The dreams won't let me sleep anymore. I'm getting sick. I can't sleep and I can't explain to anybody what's going on. Father, you've got to help me." Tom's attention was captured. Joanne had his full attention. "Dreams?" It was more of a statement than a question. "Father, I'm having dreams that have scared me half to death and when I wake up, I can't remember what the dream was about. I'm so afraid and I'm getting sick because I don't want to go to sleep and when I get to sleep I'm awakened by the dreams all night long. I'm at a loss. I don't know where to turn. You have to help me, Father. You have to help me."

Tom sat up closer to the curtained window moving to the edge of the chair. "You say you can't tell me about what the dream was, but can you tell me about the feelings you get from the dreams? Can you tell me about those feelings?"

"Father", Joanne started, "I wake up drenched in sweat. When I first wake up there is this overwhelming fear that has me crying. And when I say crying, I mean crying. Crying hysterically! I cry so hard that my whole body shakes and I am so frightened that I can't stop crying.

Father, I am always afraid and I don't know why." Tom, for the first time in over a month, was back where he should be in the confessional. He was paying attention to the needs of one of his parishioners. He was ready to offer any help he was capable of providing. He silently offered a prayer that he would be able to help this lady, but even this prayer didn't come easily.

Tom asked the questions he had been trained to ask when trying to get the base of the problem rather than the symptoms of the issue. He was hopeful that the dreams were a result of some other underlying problem and, if he was able to determine what issue or issues were bothering her, he might be able to help her.

In the middle of his questioning......Wait a minute. All of a sudden Tom remembered that he too was having dreams he couldn't remember, but were causing him a great deal of stress. He changed his line of questioning and started to ask questions that would maybe help the both of them.

"Is there anything you feel other than this fear that you are describing, anything at all from the dreams other than fear? Maybe you feel shame or disgust or a need to say you are sorry?" Tom asked a leading question because he felt a very real need to ask for forgiveness as well as the emptiness from his dreams. Maybe they shared something other than the unknown dream. Maybe they also shared the need to ask forgiveness.

"How did you know that? How could you possibly know that, Father? I didn't say anything about feeling sorry. How do you know?" Joanne was bothered that he was looking too deep into her thoughts. Immediately she felt ashamed. She had come to him to get help and maybe she was going to get that help, especially if he knew something about what she was going through, even if she didn't tell him. "I'm sorry Father. I guess I was just surprised that you knew about this other feeing I have.

I'm always saying I am sorry to God. Father, I'm saying it, but I don't know what I'm sorry about."

Tom felt a cold chill move through his body. He shivered in the dark warmth of the center confessional. "My dear friend in Christ, I, too am experiencing the very same thing you have been going through. My dreams, though I can't remember anything about them, leave me during my waking hours with a feeling of emptiness and the need to ask Our Lord for forgiveness. I can't explain this "dream thing" to you because I don't understand it myself.

But I have to tell you, we are not the only ones that this is happening to. I have a friend who told me the dreams are bothering him, too. Each one of us is experiencing the feelings from the dreams in a different way.

I feel a great emptiness, my friend feels great sorrow and you have described fear. These feelings are different and yet very similar. I want you to plan on coming back and meeting with us. Maybe if we can get together we can find a solution. I know I want to try to resolve this "dream thing" and I bet you do, too. I'm sure my friend would like the same thing." Joanne for the first time in weeks had a feeling of hope and she didn't want to let it go away without giving it her best shot. "You just tell me when and I'll be there." Father Tom Kennedy did something he had never done before, while hearing confessions, he stepped out of the chamber and met the lady in person. It was the only way he could plan a meeting with Terry and the woman. After he recorded her telephone number, and learned her name, Tom thanked her, promised that he would be in contact and stepped back into the chamber. Joanne walked out of the church still feeling a deep seated feeling of fear and a need to ask forgiveness, but there was another feeling within her very being. That was a small glimmer of hope.

Joanne walked out and Larry walked in. It had been almost a life time that Larry had been absent from the interior of any church. It was the dreams that brought him to this church now. This particular church was the place of his early Christian teachings and where his mother still went to Mass every day. He was as uncomfortable in these surroundings as he was in the wild of the BWCA when he realized all was not well in nature.

He walked gingerly to the very pew Joanne had first gone to, sat down and tried to get up the courage he would need to enter the confessional. Larry had tried everything else in his efforts to get away from the night sweats and the horror that woke him too many times a night. What was most disturbing to him was that only the portion of the recurring dream that he could remember, was the part he thought he had dealt with upon returning from the wilderness area. When he was bolted awake, sitting straight up in bed, covered in sweat, he could not remember a thing about why he was suddenly awakened. The only thing always apparent was a feeling of extreme anxiousness. He felt like he needed to plead for something to be corrected. He felt that his efforts to right this wrong were for not. Larry would wake screaming, "No! No! Please don't! Please don't!" He had no idea why he was pleading or who he was pleading with, but it was consistent. The pleading happened every time and was too many times a night now.

No matter how he tried he could never call to mind that part of the dream which always brought him out of a deep slumber. Slowly, very slowly the parts of the dream he could remember started coming back to him. He would see the birds leaving. All species of birds, big and small, dark and light, brightly colored and pale, singers and hunters would take flight and disappear out of sight over the horizon.

It was a mass exodus of birds. Larry thought that the dreams were a physiological response to what he had experienced in the woods of northern Minnesota. The experience was dramatic and very bothering to Larry. It had caused him to come close to a nervous breakdown, both in the woods and then later when he had returned to civilization.

The pictures of the birds, the animals and in particular the wolf was etched into his mind's eye and brought into vision all the time. When he least expected it, they were there. Larry thought that the endless recurring pictures in his "day-time" mind were the true cause of his nightly visions of birds in flight. He remembered the bird exodus in the dreams but not the reason the feeling of anxiousness that was always present when he was forced awake.

Larry waited until he was sure that the confessional was empty of parishioners and went into the side closest to where he had been in the pew. He knelt down on the kneeler and heard the screen window open from the other side. Larry had almost forgotten the words he had learned so many years ago that started the process of confession even thought he had no intention of using them. "Father, I once was a Catholic, but I haven't been to church for a long time. I'm not here to start going again. I need to talk to someone, and I don't know where else to go. I need help, Father."

Tom answered his plea, "How can I help you, my son?" Larry didn't really know how to answer that question without sounding like some kind of nut. Never the less he tried. "I think something is very wrong with me mentally. I have seen things that I can't explain and I don't even know if it was real. Now I'm having bad dreams about what I saw or thought I saw. The dreams are split in two. Some parts I remember, just like it happened yesterday. Some parts I can never bring to mind after the dream ends. The part I can't remember is what is the most disturbing to me even though I can't remember what it was. I wake up, out of a sound sleep, just begging for something to stop and I don't know what it is that I want to stop. I tell you Father, I'm going out of my mind. Can you help me? I've tried everything else. Do you know what is happening to me?"

Tom knew what was happening; he was having the same trouble, but didn't know why it was happening. Maybe he could find out a little more about what was common to the two of them. "Tell me what you have seen that you think is connected to your dreams." Tom asked Larry not so much as a priest but as co-sufferer. Larry told him about the wildlife that had no life to speak of and about the wolf in particular. Then he told Tom, "But Father, it isn't the birds and the wolf that is the most disturbing to me. It's the damn thing that wakes me in the middle of the night that I can't remember. It won't show itself to me and I'm going nuts because of it." Tom answered, "I know. I have the same problem. I'm awakened in the middle of the night, too. Only my dreams differ from yours because I can't remember anything about the dream but it frightens me, too."

There is more than the two of us who are having these kinds of dreams and I think if we can get together and discuss them, we can maybe find a solution. Are you open to that?" Larry had to think about that. He wasn't the type of person who enjoyed sharing his innermost thoughts. Even coming to this priest was extremely uncomfortable for him. Yet he knew he needed to do something and soon, before he truly lost his mind.

"Father, you tell me where to be and I'll be there." Tom instructed Larry to exit the confessional and give him the information he would need to contact him in the future.

Larry gave Tom a business card that he put into his shirt pocket and went back into the darkness of the little room. He looked at his watch. It was 2:00pm. He still had another hour to go before the time was up in the small chamber. This Saturday, the confessional had turned into something different than what he had expected. He wasn't really hearing the sins of his beloved parishioners but doing more of the job of a coordinator of a common problem looking for a common solution. But confession was what was on the agenda, so when he saw the red light activated by the kneeler come on, he opened the little screen window between the two chambers.

"Bless me Father for I have sinned. My last confession was two months ago. Father, I must have done something really bad but I can't think of what it was. I'm being punished. I feel like Job. He was getting it pretty bad and didn't know why either. Father, ever since my wife died I've been catchin' all kinds of hell. I don't know what to do. I don't know what I did." He could hear George crying on the other side of the darkened window.

He knew it was George because of his continuous presence at the church. George was a guy who could fix anything and there was always something for him to put back in working order in the church, the school or the rectory. George volunteered his time, now more frequent after the funeral Mass for Barbara. Tom knew that the sudden loss of his wife had been hard on George, but he didn't know that her loss had been considered a punishment by her husband. George was a strong Christian and should not have only mourned her loss, but celebrated her passing on to a "better life". Tom thought that is exactly what George was living; evidently not. Now thinking back to some of his most recent visits, Tom noticed a sort of depression and lack of humor and the smile that was always present on George's face, being absent. Tom asked, "How are you being punished. Who is punishing you?"

George responded through some tears, "God is punishing me. I've read that dreams were God's way of communicating with you. He is communicating with me every night. He is punishing me with bad dreams. I can't sleep any more, Father. The dreams are horrible and so very vivid. I dream the same thing over and over again. Every night, the same thing and I can't take it anymore, Father. I don't know what I did. Can you give me absolution and stop this horror?"

Tom was taken back. Again someone had come to the confessional who had experienced bad dreams; one right after another. This was no coincidence. Something was going on and he was going to be a very intricate part of it, but not by his own design. He was almost afraid to continue but found himself asking: "What are the dreams, George?"

Tom had used George's name, something not done in the darkened, anonymous confessional. If the confession was done in the light or face to face, the structure would have been less formal and names could be used.

George, who had experienced the sacrament all his life and who normally would have caught that the priest on the other side of the small window had used his name, was in too much distress to have noticed.

"Father, the dreams are mostly about a feeling rather than.....oh, being chased by a mad man with an axe. The feeling is so vivid when I wake up; it takes me all day long to just deal with it. I am crying all the time. I cry when I wake up and continue to cry off and on all day, until it's time to go to bed again. I'm exhausted at the end of the day and yet I don't want to go to sleep for fear of dreaming again. I'm being punished, Father and I don't why." George started crying again in the darkness on the other side of the wall.

Tom waited a little bit to allow George time to gather himself and asked, "What is the feeling that you take from the dream?" With tears still flowing George told Tom, "The feeling is of a great loss, Father. More than I ever felt when Barb died. I still miss her awfully, but this is even more overwhelming. It's different than how I felt about my wife. It's deeper and more hurtful. It's a powerful hurt in my heart. Father, it feels like I lost the very part of my soul that makes me a whole person.

Father, I hurt so badly. I don't want to feel this anymore. Make it stop." George broke down again and this time his sobbing was so horrendous the sound touched Tom's heart as well.

Tom decided to tell George about his dreams and the dreams of the others. He also arranged to get in touch with George when they all gathered for the solution meeting. The time for the Saturday confessions was now over. It was a little after 3:00pm.

When he came out of the cubical, he was surprised that the church was completely empty. The stillness inside of the large structure suddenly and without warning hit him in the face, almost striking him down. He gasped for breath and let out a moan that frightened him. The absolute emptiness was overpowering and a strange fear enveloped him completely. The church, filled or empty, had always been a place of joy and happiness to Tom, even in his youth.

Now it was a place of terror, and the terror was nothing he could rationalize. He wanted to run from the very church that he so loved just a couple of hours ago. He couldn't help himself from turning in extreme panic, run at full speed down the side isle and hurling himself at the front door. Tom flung open the two massive doors knocking a young man off his feet and onto his back.

Tom looked down at the still body of one of the high schools boys he knew as Junior Boyd. Junior's face was covered in blood, the result of an open wound located dead center in the boy's forehead. The terror Tom felt inside the church was the result of something he couldn't understand. The terror he felt now was the result of what he saw on the church steps in front of him. Tom's hurried exit had caused the door to hit the boy, knocking him to the ground. Tom knelt down beside Junior and looked closely at his chest, praying that he saw the rise and fall resulting from Junior's breathing.

Tears of relief welled up in Tom's eyes when the evidence of a breath became visible. Tom took a handkerchief from his jean's pocket and wiped the bleeding forehead, lifting Junior's head as he dabbed at the open wound.

Junior began regaining consciousness, blinking his eyes and trying to focus. "What happened?" He asked once he became somewhat awake. The priest, still trying to gather himself together, responded. "I think I must have hit you in the head with the door as I came out. I'm so very sorry Junior. I was in a hurry. I didn't mean to hurt you." "That's alright Father. Boy does my head hurt." Junior was getting to his feet while excusing Tom. "Are you sure you are okay? You blacked out and I think you should have that cut on your forehead looked at. Let me call the Doctor. I'll drive you to his office."

Junior told him that he was alright, that he had been hit harder than that in football games and he didn't want any doctor to look at a small cut. He then surprised Tom by saying, "I was coming over to talk to you anyway. I've been having some pretty bad dreams. Father, I wanted to talk to you about them." There it was again, the dreams. "What dreams, Junior?" Tom escorted the teen over to a bench in the grassy area in front of the church still dabbing at the wound. The bleeding had stopped with the slight pressure applied by the priest. He didn't want to go back into the church building to experience the terror that sent him out in a fashion that hurt this young man, so they sat together on the bench.

When he was finally sitting comfortably, Junior answered the question, "Well, I don't really know what to say. They are bad dreams but not the kind that I've told you about before." Junior was experiencing the usual sexual dreams all teenagers go through and find embarrassing to speak about. Junior was worried that he was causing the dreams himself and wanted to confess his sins.

Tom had explained to the young man that he was not a sinner but rather a normal teen who needed to pray more and try to contain his thoughts of the sex as much as he could with the help of God. Junior went on. "Father, these dreams don't have anything to do with girls. These dreams scare the hell out of me. Sorry about that Father." Junior didn't mean to cuss in front of the priest. "The dreams hit me about every night now and I think they are getting worse." "Tell me about the dreams, Junior." Tom said. "It's hard to explain, but I'll try. I wake up with a feeling of a mystery or….. no better, complete confusion.

That's it: real, complete confusion. I don't know where to go or what to do. I don't know which is right and which is wrong. I have no direction. There is no peace in me and no place for me either. I know deep inside me that my parents won't tell me what to do. I know there is no authority out there in the world. I feel really alone. I want to go and hide somewhere, but I don't know where to go. Father, in the dreams I'm running somewhere, down a long dark hallway. I'm running after something rather than from something. I don't know what it is that I'm chasing, but I do know I'll never catch whatever it is. I know that in my dream and I know it when I wake up."

Here it was again! The same "dream thing" all coming at him in one day by so many people from so many different walks of life. Tom was not as confused as Junior was but the question of "WHY?" was persistent in his mind and he had no answer. Not yet. Tom sat with Junior for a while, watching the wound on his forehead and trying to relieve him of some of the stress. Tom suggested prayer, maybe not as a solution but certainly as an aid. "It couldn't hurt." Junior said. The priest then confessed to the teenager that he, too, was having dreams. He further told Junior about some of the other people he had talked to this afternoon. Tom then asked Junior to come a meeting, not yet planned, and join the others for the purpose of finding a solution. Junior agreed.

CHAPTER NINE

THE MEETING

"Meet me in St Louie, Louie. Meet me at the fair." There are all kinds of meetings: a lodge meeting, a school board meeting, a breakfast meeting, a general meeting, a private meeting, and a stock holders meeting. A doctor's meeting is called a consultation. There is the meeting of the minds and objectives met or not met. A meeting is described as a formal assembly or a social act of getting together or a causal, unexpected encounter or a group of people coming together for one common purpose. This last description is the type of meeting that Father Tom planned. A meeting for the common purpose of helping himself and the others try to understand what the bad dreams were all about. He hoped by getting all the people who were encountering the "dream thing "together they might be able to come up with the reason and maybe even a solution. Tom's dreams had not stopped and the terrorist feelings were always present when he entered the empty church. More people had come to him with their dreams over the last week. He received phone calls from people who were parishioners as well as some whom he understood weren't even Catholic. Each conversation was followed by a suggestion they attend a short meeting in his rectory. Whenever the suggestion was voiced the response was positive. Nobody refused the invitation. The little meetings were mostly all alike. All who came to the rectory were experiencing the "dream thing" as Tom was now calling it. The dreams themselves were elusive in substance, yet all pressed the negative feelings into the dreamers' waking hours.

Tom was playing "telephone tag" with Terry. When they were finally able to connect with each other, Tom explained about his group, so he really wasn't surprised when Terry said he was putting a group together himself. Terry's group was being formed from the confessional, phone calls and from knocks on the rectory's front door. Tom explained that he had twenty-five people ready to gather and when Terry added his thirty-two, it was decided to have the meeting of the combined attendants in the basement of Terry's rectory where there was a large meeting room. It was planned for one week from the day they talked on the phone.

It was 7:00pm and the evening breeze pushed the August hot air along the cement walkway leading to the side door of the rectory at Sacred Heart Church. Tom's group would arrive between 7:30pm and 8:00PM. Tom arrived a little early to assist Terry in setting up the room for the fifty-seven expected guests. The housekeeper, Mrs. Sally Hill, had left for the day at the usual 5:00pm and the other two priests, who also called Sacred Heart home, had separate medical calls at the local hospital expecting to be gone most of the evening. Tom and Terry had the house alone for the meeting. Tom was dressed in his usual jeans and short sleeved, light blue, Roman collared shirt.

Terry was dressed more formally with the uniform of most priests his age, black pants, and a black, short sleeved, Roman collared shirt. Tom was forty-nine and Terry was sixty-seven.

Terry was always in uniform while Tom was very seldom out of his chosen cut off sweat shirt and faded jeans. Tom chose a modified priestly look for his public and private appearances. Both men were proud of their chosen profession and loved their life a priests, providing for the people around them, Catholic or not. They loved them as God loved His people.

Both men walked down the finished stairs that lead from the kitchen to the basement. The large meeting room, also finished with a drop ceiling and wood paneled walls, was used for gatherings since the house had been built so many years ago. They went to the storage closet, located off the larger room next to the stairs, getting folding chairs which they set up in a large circle around the parameter of the room. They chatted about nothing while placing the chairs. Neither man wanted to address the obvious until the others arrived. They counted the chairs only when they were all in place.

There were sixty chairs now ready for the people who were coming to the gathering. Tom asked Terry if he thought all the people who were invited would make an appearance. "Very seldom do all who were asked, come to an event. 'Many are called but few are chosen.'" Terry reminded Tom.

The doorbell rang upstairs, alerting the two priests; someone had arrived and needed admittance. Terry went upstairs, answered the door and introduced himself to one of Tom's group. Joanne arrived first, but was followed closely by two of Terry's parishioners. Terry showed them to the stairs and Tom greeted them at the bottom. It was exactly 7:30pm. From that point on there was a steady stream of arrivals, although it lasted only fifteen minutes before all who had been invited were in attendance. It was obvious that each person who arrived had a very personal issue that needed to be addressed and corrected. All were tired, all anxious, some pensive, some full of hope and others at their rope's end. There were older people like George and younger ones like Junior. There were Catholics like Joanne and people who had no religion left at all, like Larry. They were male and female, all sharing the same terror, fear and anxiety. They chose one of the chairs in the circle, sat down and remained there in utter silence. A silence that was not comfortable, yet no one broke the feeling with even a slight cough.

Terry was the last to enter the room, coming down the stairs immediately after the last guest arrived. He talked earlier to Tom about inviting a psychologist friend of his, to join the group. It was decided that the first meeting should consist of only individuals who were experiencing the "dream thing". Besides, both priests had almost as many hours in Psyche class as any of the doctors who might be invited. This was a meeting about a common problem to be shared with no one else at this time.

When Terry sat down, in the last chair available, Tom introduced himself and then Terry. Tom asked if he could start the session with a prayer and no one objected. Larry and four others from Terry's group felt a little uncomfortable about the prayer, but said nothing. Tom started, "Lord, we come to you this evening with a common problem, a dream that we do not want, a dream that we fear and don't understand. Lord, we ask you for forgiveness.

We have sinned and now we are.........." There it was again. Tom had not wanted to ask for forgiveness and had no idea where that part of his prayer had come from. He stopped the prayer and realized that all of his prayers lately, since the dreams started, had been a prayer of forgiveness. He had no reason to pray in that fashion continuously, but it always turned out that way. Some of the people he talked to about the "dream thing" told him they too were asking for forgiveness all the time and not knowing why. "I'm sorry my friends, I didn't mean to pray for forgiveness. Some of you understand that our prayers lately have all been about asking God to forgive us. We don't seem to be able to change that request. It is always there in our every attempt to talk to Him. 'Jesus, forgive me.' Is on my lips, always, and I believe it comes straight from my heart. Yet, I don't know why." Tom sat back against his chair.

"I'm doing the same thing, Father Tom, I pray all the time and all the time I'm asking God to forgive me. I'm being punished for something I did, I just don't know what. We talked about that before, when I came to you. I didn't know that you were doing the same thing with your prayers though." George was talking to Tom, but was addressing the whole group, opening the floor for the others to respond.

"Me, too!" "I'm doing the same thing." "I thought it was only me." More than half the people in the basement room spoke up, adding to the common issues and relieving some of the silent tension present. "I don't think these damn dreams are making you all feel sorry, or make you feel like you have sinned. I think they are two separate things. Two separate problems, maybe with the same origin, but not the same thing. Besides, I don't pray much anymore, although I guess I have prayed more lately." said a man named William who came to the meeting through an invitation from Terry. Seven people agreed with William, and if the truth be known, none of the seven had been praying people before the dreams.

Terry asked, "If all of our prayers are telling the Lord that we are sorry, and we don't know what we are sorry about, let's try to figure out together something we could all be collectively sorry about." Larry, who had been sitting quietly, chose this time to speak, "Is there a possibility there is something that our community or town is doing, or not doing? Or maybe the places where we meet or shop or send our kids to school? Maybe we are a part of a group of people who are guilty about something we all have a part in. I really don't know what that would be, but I'm at my wit's end with this crap." Tom answered, "Maybe you've got something there Larry. Let's all of us address the possibilities and see if any theories come out of that endeavor that we can all agree on."

Dee Dee started, "I know one thing that we are all guilty of and I've tried to do something about it. In fact, a lot of us have tried to correct, taking God out of our schools. Not long ago, I had the most disturbing, hateful night of terror I ever experienced in my life. It even made it to the newspapers across the country. I met with a group of fellow Christians and we went to a school board meeting.

When we got there, we were jumped. Some of us got hurt pretty badly. I ended up in these casts and with these crutches. It was the worst, most horrible night of my life. It was all due to us wanting to stop them from the practice of removing Our Lord from every part of our schools. That is what we are guilty about. All of us are guilty."

Tom responded, "Wow, I do remember reading about that incident. However, I don't remember the article saying anything about why the group was at the meeting. I guess that might have been not very interesting to their readers. I say that sarcastically. I can guess the real reason the media chose to neglect your true mission. The liberal media must turn their backs on anything that is not politically correct and in today's society, God is not P.C."

"Father Tom is correct," Terry injected, "there is a huge faction out there with the sole purpose of removing God from every aspect of our lives. They present themselves as the only ones who care enough to really represent the feelings of the majority of Americans. The silent majority can no longer stay silent. The vocal minority is taking over and the results of their winnings are affecting all parts of our lives today. The random killings, the school violence, the teen pregnancies, and the horrendous use of drugs are just a small indication of what happens when you take God out of the picture."

A woman named Gloria who was with Terry's group added, "I saw an e-mail yesterday called 'Mary's Little Lamb'. The whole jest of the article was what happens when Mary couldn't bring her lamb to school. Mary was the Virgin Mary and of course, the lamb was the Lamb of God. The e-mail ended with 'If you love Jesus you will send the e-mail on to other people. I didn't send it to anyone, now I feel just sick that I didn't. I'm one of the silent majority, aren't I Father?"

Tom answered, "I think that we are all a part of that silent majority. We don't object enough when we should complain loudly. We stand by and watch the slow process of the other side, taking small baby steps towards a complete take-over of our principles, morals and ethics. We all have good intentions but intentions don't get you anywhere, especially in a fight. I bet you had good intentions when you confronted the school board, didn't you?" He directed his question to Dee Dee although he hadn't met her before this night. Soon they would become close friends. All the participants of the meeting were going to become very close, very soon.

Charles, one of Tom's guests, told the group: "I'm not having the prayer problem that you are all talking about but I do have the dream thing and the feeling of being abandoned constantly with me. So, I'd like to get to the subject of the dreams, if you don't mind."

"The feeling of being left alone is driving me up a tree and that's why I came here. Father Tom told me all of you are having the dream thing, just like me, even him. Can we talk about it now, please?"

Tom responded, "That's true Charles. We are all here because of the dreams and the feelings that the dreams leave with us. I have a feeling of utter and complete darkness. It's hard to explain how darkness can become a feeling, but it does. It completely encompasses me at times. Only someone who is going through the same thing can possibly understand that the dark can bring a tremendous amount of pain with it. All of us though are experiencing pain, different pain. It is different because there are different dreams. Some of us are not able to remember the dreams, others do. As in all of our lives, each is different yet we are basically all the same."

An older man stated: "I do remember my dreams and I can tell you it isn't pleasant. I wake up every night sweating like everything. The dreams are so real that I truly believe I'm living it and it takes quite a while before I wake up enough to realize it was only dreaming. I'll tell you something else. The feelings that accompany the dreams are real enough and they never go away. I am so damn depressed, I cry all the time. I don't get much sleep anymore because I'm afraid to go to sleep. I know the dream will return. I'm tired and getting more so every day. That sure doesn't help the damn depression either. I saw my doctor about the depression and he sent me to a shrink. It just cost me money, it sure didn't help me none."

A woman who had come with her adult son spoke up: "I don't remember the dreams and neither does my son. I think we might be having the same dream though. We both wake up with the same horrible sensation that we have lost something very important and don't know where to start looking for it. We don't even know what to be looking for. It is driving us nuts. We spend all our time trying to answer the questions left by the dreams and accomplish nothing. We aren't going to work anymore, not eating half the time, just sit and try to discover what we should be looking for, what is lost. We don't have a clue where to start. We don't sleep anymore......" Her voice trailed off and she started tearing up. Her son pulled her into his arms and she melted into his hug, both of them with tears flowing.

"I feel anxious all the time." Someone told the group. Another said, "I'm feeling like I have nowhere to go and nobody cares." "I'm always mad at everyone for no good reason. I'm angry, always angry." Someone else added. "I'm so sad, I cry all the time. I can't stop crying." An older woman said," I'm so lonely all the time. I feel so utterly alone, even in a crowd. I'm so lonely right now. I'm so lonely I could cry, just like that lady and her son." And she did cry. Others joined her with their own tears.

A large black man who was a member of Terry's parish said, "I feel so anxious about something. Something is going to happen or already has happened and I can't get a hold of it. I don't know what it is or what it might be but it is destroying every part of my life. My wife couldn't stand it no more and has moved in with her sister out of town."

All around the room, in the basement of the rectory, each and every person in attendance told their own dream's aftermath. They explained what the dreams gave them: an unwelcome feeling that seemed to have no reason or explanation, no purpose other than to destroy their very lives. The product of the dreams, whether remembered or not, lasted into their days and for most, into their nights. The feelings they all

135

possessed, possessed them. They had become slaves to the emotions of the relentless dreams. Tears now filled the room as each shared their dream experience. Both women and men openly succumbed to the salty liquid dripping down their faces.

When silence once again was upon them, the uncomfortable feelings experienced in the beginning, now were missing. Their sharing and tears unified the group with an unseen power stringing them together like popcorn on a Christmas tree. Strangers, only minutes ago, were hugging each other, providing understanding and a support only each could give to the other.

Father Terry, the possessor of emptiness and lack of direction, forced himself to overcome those feelings for just a few minutes. The minutes were filled by him collecting all the emotions experienced and writing them on a piece of yellow, legal pad paper, before the emotions would force him to forget and lose interest. He walked over to Tom who had finally contained himself and handed him the paper.

Tom read the scribbling. It was more difficult reading the end of the list of "feeling words" than the beginning as Terry's concentration was slipping away the more he wrote.

Tom read the words aloud: anxious, fearful, lost, empty, sorrowful, darkness, anger, depression, loneliness, guilt, grief, suicidal, remorseful, abandoned, nervous, devastated, betrayed, numb and confused.

Terry had not been able to write all the emotions Tom read aloud. His loss of concentration hampered his efforts. Nevertheless Tom had a great number of "feeling words" in front of him and guessed at the rest of mostly illegible writing. Tom read the list aloud again. George was the first to respond. "Read them again, Father." When Tom finished with the third reading, George said," Those are most of the feelings I had when my wife died. I went through the list pretty fast though. I guess the Good Lord helped me through it. I did a lot of praying, a lot of crying and finally I got to a point of acceptance. Thank God. Those were the feelings I had though."

The woman who was with her son said: "You're right. Those are the feeling I went through when I lost my husband, William." Her son nodded his head in agreement. He, too, felt the same emotions when his dad died. An older man sitting to the right of Tom stated his reasons for agreeing with what was being stated. Soon the whole basement was full of voices in full accord, even though not everyone in attendance had lost a loved one. Even the younger members of the group, who had no personal experience with death, stated they too realized the emotions were a part of losing someone they loved.

Larry, always the thinker, said: "Loss, all the feelings of loss. You are... no we are all talking about what it feels like when we lose someone. Even the ones, who haven't had a loss because of death, are saying the same thing. It's more than losing something. We don't have all those feelings when we lose something, only when we lose someone. It's about losing someone."

Tom responded to Larry. "I think you are right, Larry, we are all talking about the emotions of loss. Now we need to figure out whom are we missing? Who is it that we are all missing in our lives? There are a lot of people here and this is not one of those games where you have to get to Kevin Bacon in eight moves. Maybe that is a thought! How can we possibly figure out who we all know, in common, and are no longer with us? I can't begin to answer that."

A man named Frank told the group, "There are too many people here to come up with an answer to that. I think we should concentrate on the dream or the prayer thing. I'm having trouble with praying too. I'm here to find out the "why" to both those questions."

Tom answered him, "Maybe the answer to those two questions is the same and the emotions are a part of that answer. I have a wild thought and maybe it is the answer to all the questions we have here tonight. Let's imagine, just for a moment, God has listened to all those people in our community who wanted Him to go away; away from our schools, away from our libraries, away from our government. Maybe He has responded to them and has gone away. He has removed Himself from our lives and will never be there for us again. I think some of us would feel that tremendous loss. Maybe we here in this room, for some reason, especially feel that loss. It may also be possible that other people in this community, or even outside this community, would feel the same tremendous loss. It is then also possible there are people who would not have those same feelings. I'm not judging. There may be various and sundry reasons they don't have the same experiences. I don't know, I'm just presenting a possible answer to the questions tonight."

Frank's wife Betty spoke up next. "If God went away all of the world would cease to be. All that "is" would disappear and we would all be gone, too. Nothing can exist without God. Our very breath is a gift from God. I don't think that is the answer to the questions tonight. I don't think we would be here asking questions if God was gone!"

Terry responded: "You're right. There would be nothing left if God disappeared. But let's take what Father Tom has said and expand on that thought. What if God has not gone away, but has just turned away. Let me explain my thought. The church speaks of a grave sin; we call it a mortal sin, and describe it as an intentional turning away from the face of God. It is a way of life, a willful and wanton life of refusing God and His graces. What would it be like if God didn't go away, He just turned away?"

Larry said: "If that were true, then we wouldn't be the only ones experiencing the "dream thing" as Father

Tom calls it. There would be a lot of Americans who would be in the same boat as us. I don't know about the rest of the world, but I do know that a lot of places in the good 'ol USA have been trying for a lot of years to kick God out. If what you say is the truth, then there are probably other places having the same type of meetings. How do we find out if that is the truth? Are other places, other people going to meetings with the same problems, the same questions? How do we find out?"

Dee Dee addressed the group, "I'm sitting here listening to the most absurd proposal I've ever heard and you people are agreeing with this ridiculous premise. I've fought for years against the establishment and their attempts to remove God from our everyday lives. I've been beaten, broken and cursed for bringing it into the light of the public eye. I've been on the verge of calling an end to my crusade and just continuing on my merry way. Then someone says something or someone does something and I'm back on my bandwagon. I know what it is to fight and not see any apparent results for my efforts. I was beginning to think it was a lost cause or a fight that would never be won. Now you are telling me that the other side has already won. That is a thought I will not harbor in my heart. I will not accept that most horrible consideration. I will not!"

Tom answered her, "It is only horrible if we do nothing about it. If this is the reason we are all here tonight then the direction we must take is in front of us. We must turn

His face back to us and then we must continue the fight that Dee Dee has started. We must band together and reverse the way things are right now. It is all beginning to make sense to me. We have to get together and continue the fight. Don't you see? Somehow we must all let God know we are together and willing to fight for Him. All we want is to have Him turn back towards us. We are His children and He is our father. He must not turn away from us and we must find a way to let Him know how much we need Him. Now I know what my prayers have all been about. Don't you see? I am so sorry I haven't done enough to stop the establishment and join the fight. I'm sorry I let Him turn His face away from us. I'm so sorry."

George said, "That makes sense. That's why I feel like I'm being punished. I am not being punished, but I know why I feel like I am. I didn't do enough either. That is going to change right now. My wife always tried to get me to go to those meetings and voice our objections to what they were doing, but I never went. I always said I had more important things to do. I have no idea what could have been more important than this right now.

Can you imagine having something more important that telling them to leave God alone? Maybe I'm not being punished, but I'm as sorry as Father Tom, over there, that I didn't do anything. That will change."

Larry added, "I had a strange thing happen to me up north, in the wilderness. I went camping and when I got there everything was wrong. I saw things I still don't believe nor understand today. I saw stuff that almost drove me crazy. In fact, I did almost go insane for a time and had a nervous breakdown. The doctors told me what I saw was nothing more than my imagination. But I know better than that. I saw birds and animals just standing around, doing nothing. I saw a wolf drown because it wouldn't even try to swim: it just sank in the water until it was out of sight. I tried to save it, but I couldn't. It just sank. It was the most disturbing thing I have ever been witness to in my life. Maybe it happened because God turned away from them, too. What did they ever do to deserve that? I don't know, but some of this stuff is falling into place like a jigsaw puzzle, at least to me. I'm not a religious man, but I do accept there is a God. If He is real then some of this stuff we are all talking about could be because of Him. I was taught in grade school that He was a loving God. If that is true, then why does He not love us? Why is He punishing us? Why are we going through this torture? "

Sgt. Juan Lopez, for the first time tonight, spoke to the group. "You are talking about birds, animals, and wolves. I saw human beings turn into animals and they didn't just stand around doing nothing either. I'm a police officer and was working the 'weekend of terror' as the newspapers called it. I call it a weekend from hell. I don't know why it started or why it ended. All I do know is: I saw people do things that were insane, destructive, just plain nuts. They were out of their minds. I had two officers die the first night. One of them shot the other and then killed himself. There was death all over the place. There were so many killings that we couldn't come up with a death count for two days. This gentleman here said that he saw things that almost drove him crazy in the wilderness, well, let me tell you something: You didn't see anything, Mister! I saw things that no human being should ever see and I lost it. I ended up in the loony bin too. I was in the hospital for two months and so were other people, some cops, some firefighters, some citizens. We were all there because of that weekend.

I'll tell you all something else. There was no God there that weekend. No God at all. I'm a cradle Catholic but I lost all my faith over that Saturday and Sunday. I don't believe any God would have allowed that carnage. I've seen a lot of crime over the 15 years on the street, but not anything like that. You talk about God turning away from us, well I say God is dead or never has been alive."

Harold came with his wife, Mary, from Tom's parish. "I know what he means. I feel the same way. I saw the reports on the TV and then drove downtown that Saturday night. What I saw happening to our city was like the devil had unleashed all his demons and they were eating my neighbors alive. If there is a God, what I saw could not have happened.

They weren't human. I don't know what they were, but they weren't human beings. The rage and fury in their eyes was not of this world. The people were no longer people. I saw them change. Then I saw them change back right before they died. It was the most bizarre sight imaginable. They went from raging maniacs to docile morons oblivious to the mayhem they had just caused.

Then one of the others would kill them. If God was a part of that, then my understanding of who He is has been all wrong. I feel the same way as that cop over there. There is no God."

Terry answered, "I'm a priest. My business is God stuff. I think I have probably questioned His existence more than anyone in this room, with the exception of Father Tom and only because I'm older than him. I think we who have "the life calling" seem to question our faith a lot and I truly believe that the questions have reinforced my faith. I have a stronger faith than if I hadn't questioned it at all. It's being tested all the time. Anyone who doesn't question their faith isn't living their faith. My father was not a Catholic; in fact he wasn't a very religious man at all. He was a man of a very deep faith though and it was his influence that made me question all the aspects of my faith. When I was a kid, I would go to him to share a new revelation I had discovered about my religion and he would simply say to me, 'prove it'. I have been proving it to myself ever since. What we experienced, each one of us, would surely make us all question our spiritual beliefs. I have successfully answered most of the questions to myself;

I have answered the major question about God's existence to myself and can say that I believe He is alive and well, though I'm not sure about the wellness. Not right now. But I'm sure He is alive. What some of you have offered as an answer to the situation we all have been through is something that has touched a chord in my heart and mind. If God has turned His face away from us then we are experiencing only His back. Remember the bible story about the woman who was hemorrhaging and thought that if she could just touch the garment, that Jesus wore, she would be healed. Her faith in Jesus cured her. If we have faith enough to believe: if we could only touch His back, we could change everything, our faith might be enough to do just that. Maybe we have found the answer. I'm not sure how to go about it though. I certainly have never addressed anything like this before, so I have no point of reference to fall back on. I don't know how to guide any of you. I don't know what to do myself."

Tom said, "I'm in full agreement with you Terry. I've checked my faith many times, especially over the last few weeks, and still I believe in God. I also have to agree with Father Terry, God may not be well. Well, in a manner of speaking. I can't claim to understand all the aspects of God's being, so I won't even try. I do believe though He has given us enough intelligence to make free will decisions and live the results of those decisions. I know we, as a society, have made some pretty bad decisions and the rest of us haven't done enough to change those positions. If God is responding to the free will of those in our society who have tried to remove any reference to Him, then I believe it is possible that God could still exist and in some way has turned away from us. I don't fully understand how that is possible.

I do believe if He turned away from us and left us alone, we would not be here to address these questions. We would not exist. He still loves us, so if He has turned away He has turned with a heavy heart. He is still our father. So He must still be available to us in some manner. I don't know what we can do to change what has happened except through prayer and right now I can't even pray the way I want to. The way He taught us. Maybe that is part of what is going on though? Like Father Terry said: We don't know what to do, we have never been in this situations before."

George suggested, "Maybe you should get the diocese involved. I bet the Bishop could help. I've met him before and he sure seems like the kind of guy who would be glad to tell you what to do. Oh, that sounded wrong! I meant to say that he seems the type of guy who would help you, if you asked him. Am I right?"

Tom answered, "Both Father Terry and I have been in contact with the Bishop. He is very much aware of these meetings and the problems we all share. He wanted us to report back to him when the meeting was over. He is very supportive and will have a lot of involvement after tonight, after this meeting. He can better direct us after he hears what, if anything is accomplished tonight."

A man named Buck, looking more like a biker than someone who was in attendance at a meeting of this kind said, "I'm not like you people. I can tell that most of you here lead a good life. I think most of you have some kind of religious background. I haven't had any and I don't live a good life. I guess you would all call me a sinner. My neighbor lady and I were talking about these damn dreams and she insisted that I come here tonight with her. She's a good woman. She belongs here, I don't. I shouldn't be here. I'm not like you. I don't know what I'm doing here. I can't understand what you all are talking about. You over there, talk about not believing in God. I've never even thought about it. And you told us that you believe God is punishing you. I make my own punishment. I punish the ones I want to. I don't rely on any God, I do it myself. I'm having the dreams you all are talking about, but I don't believe it has anything to do with any God. I don't know what I'm doing here."

Terry responded, "Just because you don't believe in Him doesn't mean that He doesn't believe in you. It is said that 'Jesus didn't come to earth for the righteous. He came for the sinners.' If you really think you came here on your own, or because of your neighbor's invitation, then I think you are missing something very important. Maybe more than you believe, your presence here is the most important thing I've become aware of tonight. It means that God has not completely turned away from us yet. You may not agree, but I believe He had a major part in getting you here with us. You belong here. Oh yes, you belong here. And I, for one, am glad you came."

Buck just settled back into his chair and appeared resolved to the fact they all believed he was supposed to be one of the group meeting in the basement of the rectory. With a lot of answers proposed, but none of the resolutions provided, the meeting seemed to be coming to an end. Both priests thanked the group for coming and promised to follow up with the Bishop. Then they promised to call each of them and keep them informed. All the people left quietly with feelings that their problems, their dreams, their anxieties, their fears had been addressed but certainly not resolve. It was 10:00pm

CHAPTER TEN

BISHOP MICHAEL BLOM

om drove over to the rectory and picked up Terry. The two priests drove together to meet with the Bishop. Bishop Michael Blom was a no nonsense kind of leader with a thread of compassion woven throughout the whole garment of his personality.

He smiled a lot and was easy to joke with. His faith was lived every day. He was a true example of the reflection of Christ's face. All believers wanted to exhibit this same quality. When it came to matters of the diocese, he was a strong director of the clergy assigned to him. He listened well and when appropriate gave sound advice and direction. His job, as the center figure of the twenty six parishes assigned to him, was difficult and, at times, almost more than one man would want to take on as a profession. Mike didn't think of his work as a profession though, more of a "calling". Mike Blom was a priest first and an administrator second. That meant his first calling to become a religious was primary. So directions he gave to the priests were always tempered within his early teachings from the seminary, which included among other studies, psychology. The priests found him to be understanding and at the same time, strong in his commitment to lead. He was an easy man to bring your troubles to.

The housekeeper, Mrs. Irene McIntosh a stately, round woman in her early seventies, escorted the two priests to where the Bishop was in the study, which he used as an office. Both Tom and Terry were surprised to see fifteen other priests in the study. All the priests knew each other and hugs of greeting were exchanged. Some pleasantries were shared, but the atmosphere in the room was solemn, something wasn't right.

Mike started the meeting, "I know that most of you didn't expect to see the others here. I didn't expect to have all the calls I got this week. I finally surmised that all of us are experiencing the same serious situation in our parishes. You have reported dreams of terror that not only your parishioners, but you, too, are living with. You have all told me that your prayer life and that of your flocks, have changed. I called you all here to compare notes and try to come to some conclusions which I can take to the Cardinal. So please make yourselves comfortable, I think we might be here for a while."

Mrs. McIntosh brought in coffee, soft drinks, ice glasses and cups, setting it all on the center table in the study. Nothing was said until she left the room. Then Tom started, "Terry and I met with about 50 people in his rectory basement. The meeting got pretty intense. The stories shared, led us in a direction that we finally concluded was a possible reason all this crap is happening, but this sounds a bit crazy.

We had a partial consensus that God is probably having a definite influence on this situation. We further decided that He could be turning away from us. Let me explain where this thought came from.

We, as a society, as you all know, have very diligently tried to remove any reference to God, Christian or not, from all aspects of our public lives.

The public schools, the government buildings, the sports games have all been places where they have been successful in removing God. I have even heard of a bill in front of Congress that would remove all the evangelists from radio and television. The bill would also remove any reference to Christmas, including the music. If we have, in fact, asked long and loud enough for Him to get out and the rest of us haven't done enough to change their intent, then maybe He has responded to their wants and needs. Maybe God has turned His face away from us."

Father Quinton Thomas, the assistant from Guardian Angels Parish told the group of priests, "I can't believe that our group came to the same conclusion as yours. Bob and I also had a group meeting at our rectory. They all came to the same conclusion; that God is missing.

He has turned His face away from our society. This is crazy." Father Bob Jones was the Pastor at St Mary's of the Lake Parish. Bob said, "This is more than a little crazy, Q. This is some serious business. When more than 100 people can meet in two different places and come up with something as farfetched as God turning His face away from us, it scares the hell out of me. Are we all losing our minds? Okay, yes our group did think that God was missing. They also wanted to make it clear that they thought He wasn't gone, only missing. This notion is against everything I have ever been taught or believed in. Yet here we are, and from the nodding heads in this room, I can see this group is in full agreement. There is something very wrong with what we are all talking about and agreeing with. I admit it's more than a coincidence but I don't know what to call it. I'll tell you this, my priestly brothers, I am really scared."

Father Phillip Kane from Christ the King Parish said, "What happens if God is going to do more than turn His face away from us? What happens if He turns completely away from us? I'll tell you what! We cannot exist. We will no longer be and I mean our souls as well. God is our life and if we throw Him away completely and He responds completely.....What happens? You all know what happens! I agree with you Bob, I am scared as hell, too."

Terry asked, "Mike, have you been in touch with James Cardinal Roan about this?

The Bishop responded, "Not yet Terry. I wanted to get you all together first, before I go to him with what you describe as a 'farfetched' story. It all sounded crazy to me, too, when you first started calling. Now it is a major concern, not only for you but for the whole church. From this get together, I can present a firsthand report to His Eminence. I need all the information I can get before I tell him what we think is going on.

If he hasn't heard it from some other place or other people I might have a hard time convincing him. I'm not sure that I'm totally convinced. You are asking me to tell the Cardinal that you collectively think that God has turned His face away from His people.

You have all come to the same conclusion by having group meeting with people who have come to you, complaining that they are having bad dreams and a troubled prayer life. I don't believe that I can possibly go to him with what you have given me so far. So let's continue with this information meeting. Try to convince me."

Father Raymond Sharpener of Holy Trinity responded, "Convince you? I can't convince myself. I know in my heart this stuff is real and what we suspect is true, but my mind won't accept the premise. My 40 some years as a diocesan priest won't let me accept that Our Lord has turned away. All that I have taught the seminarians all these years is in stark contrast to what I am now living. How do I convince you, Mike, when I can't talk myself into believing? When I met with my people and heard their stories, I was flabbergasted. The stories they told me about their horrible dreams and their lack of sleep, rang a terrible bell with me. Mike, I, too, am having these dreams. Dreams so disturbing that they followed me into the day light hours. Dreams whose content I can't recall when awake. All the dreams that we talked about at our meeting had the emotions of loss connected to the horror. All the priests, here in this room, have dealt with the emotions of loss, the tears of separation from loved ones. We have all celebrated funeral masses, and yet we also know this loss is different. This loss is severe. It is a loss that goes to the very depth of our souls. We can't go on living this way. There has to be something we can do. I would have suggested prayer first to anybody who came to me with massive problems, but our prayers have taken a different direction and I don't believe God is listening to our prayers any more. Even the masses I celebrate have become different. I no longer find the joy in the celebration. They seem empty. I don't know how to explain it, but I no longer enjoy the mass. We need some direction, if not from you Mike or the Cardinal then maybe from the Pope himself. With a situation this grave I wouldn't be afraid to ask Rome for help."

All the priests in the study reflected the same message to each other and to the Bishop. The messages included their dreams, their prayers and the masses they celebrated. When all had their opportunity to vent, Mike Blom sat back in the overstuffed high back chair that was his favorite place to park while in the room. He would often find himself in the dark red chair with a book late at night. One of the assistant priests would wake him when their day was ending, so the whole night wouldn't be spent with the Bishop sleeping in the chair. "My brothers in Christ, I think I have enough understanding of what you and your parishioners are going through to call His Eminence in the morning. I fully agree that this matter must be addressed right away and if needed maybe the best direction would be to go to Rome, which would be James' decision. The issues that you have brought to me are as foreign to me as they must have been to you when it all started. The only difference is that I have not experienced any of these symptoms myself.

I can understand your frustrations, in a very limited way. I can't accept that all of you, my friends, believe God has somehow turned a deaf ear to His people. I cannot accept it myself, but also cannot discard that you all are firm in your belief.

I know each of you and have a great deal of love and respect for you all. For this reason I will explain to James exactly what you have told me. I'll call you together again after our meeting. I would normally ask you to pray for me, but for what you have said, I probably wouldn't get those prayers. So, I'll pray for you, your people and me instead."

Rabbi Phil Golden was meeting with a group from his synagogue, both men and women. The people had come to his house and were trying to get comfortable in the living room. The house was not that big and the 45 people who had arrived at 6:30pm were pretty well jammed into the largest room in the home. Some of the younger people were sitting on the floor, older ones seated on chairs and couches. Some of the dining room and kitchen chairs had been moved into the living room. Every possible sitting space was being utilized. Ruth Golden, always the gracious hostess, served finger food and wine to all who wanted it. Phil started the session by saying, "I have asked you all here for the purpose of determining what the hell is going on."

There was some snickering, but mostly the light hearted attempt was met with silence. Phil always tried to interject some lighter substance in any of his formal presentations. It didn't work this evening. He continued, "At one time or another, within the last two weeks, you have all come to me for spiritual guidance. That is my job and I'm generally very good at it, but this time I find I am at a loss. I have never encountered the problems you have present to me. The situations you explain to me are all exactly the same as your neighbors' who are with us here tonight. So, not only are your problems the same for each of you, they are different from anything I have ever encountered before. The spiritual guidance you are asking for is beyond my ability. I don't know how to advise you. I don't know what God wants of us, wants of me. Maybe if we share we can come to a solution to the problems you all are experiencing."

The horrible dreams were shared, the changed prayer life was shared and the horrendous feelings of loss were shared. Sometime during the next three hours their sharing brought them to a conclusion, the same conclusion that the Catholics came to during their group meetings. The Jewish religion, so steeped in tradition and history, could not allow for the conclusion agreed upon at this evening. Each individual Jewish man and woman there had to come to grips with their understanding of the passage in the Torah that addresses God never leaving His people alone. In Hebrews 13:5 it is written: *'I will never leave you or forsake you.'* So each man and woman there concluded that God had not forsaken them but had somehow turned His face away from them. The concept was difficult to understand, much less accept, but once the stories all came out into the stark light of reality, there was no denying that obvious conclusion.

The night ended about 9:30pm with each member walking quietly to their vehicle, not at all satisfied with the outcome of the gathering but resolved to the outcome. Plans had been made to come together again after some time had passed and the Rabbi could soak in the information just heard from his flock.

All Christian denominations: The Lutherans, Methodists, Baptists, Church of Christ, Episcopalians, Presbyterians, Mormons and Nazarenes were meeting the same week for the same reasons. Non-Denominational Christian churches were in the basements and small buildings where they gathered on Wednesday nights and Sunday mornings and Non-Christian believers: Muslims, Buddhists, Hindus, were also meeting in their mosques, temples and homes. All who believed in God were meeting because they didn't understand what was happening to them.

They were suffering from the bad dreams, the loss of sleep and their prayer life had taken such a strange turn. None of this could be endured by the faithful any longer. They couldn't understand it, they couldn't endure it, they needed help and guidance from their religious leaders and the leaders couldn't offer them any help, any answers. The leaders were as helpless as any of their followers. All religious communities, without their guidance and directions, were in a state of turmoil, chaos and extreme unrest.

As each leader went to present their concerns to their superiors, so did Bishop Michael Blom. He entered the Cardinal's office. Only the two men would be there for this initial meeting. If the session would warrant it, more of the church's hierarchy would be called to a follow-up meeting. To show respect for the position of Cardinal, Mike knelt and kissed the ring on James Roan's right hand, ring finger. After the formalities of a proper greeting were exchanged, Mike sat in a chair positioned in front of the desk.

James pulled up a high backed, desk chair and leaned forward to hear what Mike had alluded to on the phone, when he called to arrange for this meeting three days ago. But first he said, "Michael, you sounded so concerned when you called. I'm sure we can get to the root of this and nip it in the bud, before it gets out of hand. We've worked out situations together before and I sure we can handle this just fine by working together again. Let's not blow this out of proportion, Michael."

Mike sat back in the chair, deflated. He got shot down before he even started. The Cardinal had no idea of what Mike had seen and heard from the group of priests for whom he had a tremendous amount of respect. To blow off their suffering before he had even had an opportunity to hear what Mike had to say, not only discouraged the Bishop, it infuriated him. "Damn it Jim, this isn't something to push under the rug. It is very serious or I wouldn't be here in such a hurry or with such a concern. Yes, we have done a good job before in hiding or correcting situations, but this is not like before and I need you to get on board with me. And I sure don't need you to push me out the door before I even get started."

James responded, "Holy cow Mike, I don't think I ever saw you like this before. Okay, you have my undivided attention, that's for sure. But you told me, on the phone, some of your priests were having bad dreams and trouble with praying. You have to understand how that sounded to me.

If there is more to it than that, I'm willing to listen. I'm sorry if I gave you the impression that I don't care. I do care, about all the priests and you too, Mike."

Still frustrated with the Cardinal's lack of concern, Mike told him, "It is a lot more than some priests having bad dreams. It's a whole hell of lot more than that. It's all kinds of people, clergy and lay alike; who are having, not bad dreams, but horrible, tormenting, hideous day and night turmoil resulting from their slumber. So horrendous are the effects from these dreams that they cannot allow themselves to sleep. When they finally succumb to the need for rest, they are awakened by the terror of the dreams. Some remember the dreams, but most only recall a feeling described as a tremendous loss and we can't recall why."

James responded, "You are very upset. You said that "WE can't recall why". Mike, are you having these dreams too?

"I wasn't before they came to see me. I told them that I couldn't do their concerns justice, because I wasn't experiencing the dreams myself. I was worried that I might not bring their feelings to you as I needed. I prayed about that, like I told them I would, and my prayers turned into an act of contrition. All of a sudden I was praying for forgiveness and I couldn't change that. James, that night I had one of the dreams and have had them ever since. I can't remember what the dreams are about, but I wake with the feeling of being completely and totally alone.

The emotions stay with me all the time. I can't get rid of it. I am so lonesome I cry most of the time. I can't take care of my responsibilities because of the constant crying. I'm not the kind of man who cries, but I'm crying all the time. I want so desperately to be with someone, but I don't know who. I've lost both my parents long ago but somehow the feeling of being alone brings them to mind. I'm not saying that I miss them. I'm missing someone else, but somehow they are tied to the loss. I've not been able to sleep. The terror of having the dream again is too much. Like I told you, when I finally fall asleep, I wake up with the horror of that tremendous loss and each time it is worse. And James, I can't pray anymore. All my attempts turn to cries of forgiveness. I want forgiveness, but for what, I do not know."

James said, "I'm so sorry, I didn't see the stress in your face before. I was too preoccupied with attempting to discourage you from what I thought was nonsense. I now can see how much distress you are in and I truly want to help. I want to help, not only you, but if all the other priests and parishioners are having the same trouble, I want to help them too. Michael, tell me what you want me to do."

At this point the bishop broke down and while tears flowed down his cheeks he told the Cardinal, "I don't know! I don't know what you can do. That's why I'm here. That's why the priests came to me. We don't know what to do. Jim, you have got to help us."

CHAPTER ELEVEN

ONE NATION UNDER GOD

"One Nation Under God." "Our Nation was founded with Judeo-Christian principals." "In God We Trust"

Our forefathers did not, by accident, bring God into the design of our government. Read the Preamble of the Constitution, The Constitution itself and the Bill of Rights; these documents will provide enough evidence to the reader that any question of God being a part of our founding fathers' intent, was not an accident.

"It is impossible to rightly govern the world without God and the Bible." (George Washington, Father of our country.)

"Freedom is not a gift bestowed upon us by other men, but a right that belongs to us by the laws of God and nature." (Benjamin Franklin, signer of the Constitution and Declaration of Independence.)

Benjamin Rush, a signer of the Declaration of Independence, put it this way:

"By renouncing the Bible, philosophers swing from their moorings upon all moral subjects. . . . It is the only correct map of the human heart that ever has been published. . . . All systems of religion, morals, and government not founded upon it [the Bible] must perish, and how consoling the thought, it will not only survive the wreck of these systems but the world itself."

If thou wouldst rule well, thou must rule for God, and to do that, thou must be ruled by Him....Those who will not be governed by God will be ruled by tyrants. (William Penn, founder of Pennsylvania.)

Have we in the United States come so far away from what they wanted of us? Have we Americans been reluctant to oppose the thought behind statements like: "God should be taken out of our country's fabric, because not everyone believes in it and thus the laws and values of one religion should not be given power over others." Or "The absence of religion is a lot less offensive than the presence." Can all Americans be at blame for allowing the government to throw God out of the public buildings? Should we, as the church, or as individuals, done more to stop the trend set in motion by the atheists? Why has the U.S.A. drifted away from the design on which our country was founded; that God is intentionally deep within the fabric of our government?

These were thoughts that pounded in the head of James Cardinal Roan as he reclined in bed, trying to get Father Mike out of his mind, so he could sleep. Could Mike be right and God had turned His face away from His people, His church? Mike was not the kind of man who James found to be an alarmist, in fact pretty much the opposite.

He and Mike had worked on a couple of problems within his diocese dealing with, among other things, complaints about priests.

One complaint was from a parish council who told the Bishop that their priest was a dictator who wouldn't listen to any suggestion presented to him by the council. The Cardinal and the Bishop met with the priest and successfully brought him off his pedestal by being sympathetic to his views and listening to his complaints about the large family who thought they were the ones who really ran the parish. The council wanted the priest removed from their church and wanted a say in who was sent as a replacement. The council was also soothed by Mike when he explained to them that there was a shortage of priests and they would be without one until the next graduating class from the seminary. He told them that they were lucky they had a priest at all and if he was removed they would become a mission parish, where a priest would only visit and not take up residency. The council's members agreed the answer to their problem was to have the priest talked to and stay rather than the alternative. All parties were content at the end of the sessions.

James had a lot of confidence in the Bishop, so the problem as presented to the Cardinal, although farfetched as it sounded, he had to consider. It was this reflection of the problem that kept him awake. Could it be possible? Although all the people who had been meeting came up with the same conclusion, was there something else at play here, something evil? Should he consider that pure evil was somehow responsible for the believer's pain and suffering? Mike was so sure that all the problems were due to the actions of God, and Mike had been a recipient of the pain and suffering, but only after he needed to understand. Was it God's intent to let Mike endure the same as the others, so he could be a better presenter to James? James had to consider that maybe the devil's actions were involved. Yet, how could all the individuals who attended the many meetings be so sure that it was God's actions without even considering the opposite? The Native Americans called him the *Trickster;* The Christian faiths called him a liar, the Bible had many names for him but it all came down to one thing: the Opposite of God would use any trick to take souls away, especially a great huge lie. James had to think over all possibilities.

The Cardinal finally drifted off to sleep about 2:00am. It was a fitful night, full of horrendous dreams that woke him several times before the alarm clock went off at 6:00am, announcing the end of his slumber. When he reached over to push the button that would silence the alarm, he noticed that the sleeve of his night shirt was wet.

When he pulled back the covers he realized he had been sweating so profusely that, not only were his pajamas soaked, but most of the bed sheets as well. What was it that had caused such an abnormal bath in the middle of the night? James couldn't remember anything about the night other than he had awakened a number of times by what he assumed were bad dreams.

He couldn't bring to mind any of the substance of the dreams, so he didn't know why his sleep was disturbed; only that it had been. He immediately thought of the "dream thing" as Mike had called it and tried to put into perspective if he felt the presence of Lucifer or not. He didn't. He went directly to his knees beside the bed and started to pray. His prayer was simple and his words direct. He asked God, through the Spirit, to answer his question: *"Was this dream thing related to God or the devil?"*

His answer was immediate. James Cardinal Roan, in the middle of his short prayer, started asking God to forgive him.

He pleaded that his lack of faith to be forgiven, his doubting in the power of God to be forgiven, his worldliness pushing aside his spiritual life to be forgiven and most of all his non-acceptances of the truth laid at his feet, that God had turned His face away, to be forgiven.

James lay prostrate on the floor of the bedroom and cried like a baby. So many of the individuals who had attended the meetings had reported their prayer life being turned into something they didn't understand, something uncontrollable, something of an act of contrition they hadn't started, but ended with. Some reported that they were being punished for something, but had no idea what they had done. They prayed for forgiveness, but didn't know why. James knew why. He had prayed for an answer to his most pressing question and got the answer. It was as clear to him as it was vague and unclear to the others. They didn't know why; he did. Because his prayer had been answered, there was now direction he must take.

A whole week passed and the phone in his study had more use than ever before. There were as many calls in, as there were calls out. Exactly one week and one day later he called his staff together for a short prayer and meeting. James knew that any prayer he would offer would come out as a prayer of requested forgiveness, so he asked Father William (Billy) Thompson to say it. James had directed him to say a prayer asking God's blessing for the pathway on which they were about to embark. Billy didn't know the direction or the purpose of the proposed "pathway", so he said a very generic prayer. James then asked his staff to take a seat and get ready for the most disturbing information they would ever hear.

"What I'm about to tell you is going to sound like I'm out of my mind. I had real doubts myself when I first became aware there was something amiss. The Bishop came here last week, I'm sure you all know that. What you don't know is why he was here. Most of the time my staff is involved from the get go.

This time it was different because I wasn't sure I was going to believe Mike, though I have a tremendous amount of respect for him. My friends in Christ, I should have never doubted him.

Mike came here to tell me about the people in his diocese, both the clergy and laity, who were experiencing some very strange happenings. At pretty much the same time they were all having very bad dreams. Some of them could remember what the dreams were about, some couldn't. But, each and every person knew that the dreams left them with a tremendous feeling of loss. These feelings should not be taken lightly; they were so intense that all experienced sleep deprivation and extreme depression. Some reported crying all the time and I'm not exaggerating. I have experienced some tears myself. But I'll get into that later. The people who were having trouble sleeping, because of the dreams, also reported a change in their prayer life. It should be noted that not all of the people who were having trouble with their prayers....prayed regularly. These people were not exactly the chosen people, but more of your every day, run of the mill kind.

Not all were Christian. Not all were Jewish. I can say this, not because of what the Bishop told me, but what other leaders of other denominations have told me this week.

I have made and received numerous calls from the Jewish and Muslim communities as well as a whole lot of calls from other Christian faiths. The calls were all the same, the membership was having horrible dreams and extreme depression followed by a change in their prayers. The changed prayer life is described as what the Catholic Church calls an Act of Contrition. They could not change that. All the prayers turned into requests of forgiveness and consistently they didn't know what they had done to require forgiveness. I have experienced this conundrum myself and again, I will get to that later.

Another thing was common to most of the troubled believers. Nature was not acting in a normal way. Some reported animals and birds being despondent in very peculiar and excessive manners. The gardens, the trees and flowers were not right. The changes in nature became another clog in the wheels that drove these people to the edge. It took them to medical and mental doctors. It took them to their religious leaders for relief of the constant reminder of the abnormalities they had seen and experienced. Nature not acting right almost drove them insane.

The most disturbing of all the changes is what we humans have done to each other. The senseless taking of life and the meaningless destruction of property, by mindless people has taken place in most of our large cities. The gathering of crowds and the forming of riots in our streets, destroying all in their path, has been reported by all the media throughout all of America. This must not to be taken lightly. When people lose their own humanity and act in a manner that not even the animals would consider, we must be alert and question why.

When the leaders received all this knowledge from their flock or experienced it themselves, they called meetings. The purpose of these meetings was simply to compare experiences and try to determine what was happening and why. Consistently they all came to the same conclusion. Now try to put this into perspective: thousands of people coming together from different faiths and cultures, all coming up with the same conclusion. What I'm going to tell you now is not said lightly or without considerable investigation into all possibilities surrounding the "dream thing", as Mike calls it.

My brothers in Christ, it is our collective opinion that God has turned His face away from His people. God has not forsaken His people, He has not departed and He is alive though some think Him dead. I know these things because I have had experiences myself. I, too, lived through the dreams. Dreams that I could not recall when I woke up, but had a very real effect on me during the night. The night after the Bishop's visit, the bed I sleep in and the bed clothes I wore were soaked clear through with my own perspiration when I awakened. Whatever the dreams were had me sweating profusely. The dreams left me with a tremendous feeling of loss.

I was frightened and went immediately to my knees. I said a prayer I never thought I would ever utter. I asked to know if this entire "dream thing" was a result of God's doing or if there was the evil influence of the devil at work. That prayer, of unintended attrition, answered my plea to understand. Billy that is why I asked you to say that prayer before this meeting, I know that my prayers had been changed overnight. I could no longer pray what I had intended.

I was given an answer that confirmed all the conclusions drawn by so many others who were and are suffering like I am now. God has turned away from us and we must turn Him back. We cannot continue to exist without God looking over us.

I am also convinced that His turning away is directly the result of what we here in the United States have done or failed to do. For a long time now we have pushed God farther and farther out of our lives. It started a long time ago with the term 'Politically Correct'. We were particularly interested in not offending anybody and not at all concerned that we were offending our God. The atheists had to have their way and we allowed that to happen without a concern about God having His way.

Our government had to assure its citizens there would be a separation of church and state by removing our national motto, 'In God We Trust', from public view. Some of our currency no longer contains those precious words, our public buildings have had the Ten

Commandments taken down. We have lost sight of what the Constitution was designed to mean by the phrase: "Separation **of** church and state". The meaning is now, "Separation of church **from** state". There can be no mention of prayer in our schools or school events. Our forefathers did not intend this to happen.

It was their intent to design our government with God in every particle of the fabric that makes us united, that makes us great. We are no longer great and we are no longer united. What our founding fathers provided for us, is now lost.

What they put in place has been replaced and it is everyone's fault, everyone who claims to be an American. America has forced the face of God to turn away from it.

We are the United States and we can unite. More importantly, we are the believers and we can call the believers together. The first steps have already been provided for us. Other faith communities are starting the process the same as we are today. Any actions we take must be approved by the Vatican and yet I'm not sure how they are going to receive this information. I wasn't sure how you here were going to receive it. Deep in my heart I know the truth and I know we have to take on the burden of rectifying what we have let go. I have my ideas of what must be done so I'm now asking you for your questions. I need your voices, your concerns now."

Billy sat up straight in his chair; he had a tendency to slouch, and asked, "The Trinity. The Father, Son and Spirit, have they all turned away from us? When you speak of God do you mean the God-Head or The Three in One?"

The Cardinal replied, "I don't have a complete answer to that. I **do** know that the Trinity cannot be in conflict with each other. As I understand God to be, I think that all three persons of the Holy Trinity will accept that which affects one, affects all. Yet, when I prayed I invoked the Holy Spirit, through Jesus' name, to provide me with His gift of understanding, my prayer was answered. The Son calls on His humanity for the experience of the Trinity so Jesus' influence will guide us in our efforts to bring the Trinity's collective face back to us. I'm not trying to indicate that Jesus is separated from the Father and Spirit, but rather to say that His time on earth, as human, will help direct us. The Trinity will act as one no matter what we on earth try to do to change that. Not all the world's religions accept the Trinity, so they can't ask the same question that you just did.

However, the Christian churches I talked with this week, have all reported the same thing with their followers. So. I have to say to you Billy, I don't know, but reason dictated all three in one, have turned away. "

The youngest of the staff assigned to the Cardinal, Father Francis Simon asked, "Are you telling us that we have to believe what you have just told us as a matter of faith or are we open to our own interpretation of the events?"

"Fran, you can be your own person in this dilemma. I suggest that you open your heart and mind to what has been presented to you though. I doubted at first myself and I assure you I do not doubt now.

The power of our God is still very strong and the answer to my prayer has been anything but a blessing to me, if there is anything that I have been blessed with from all of this, it's in believing in the truth. You can believe or you can doubt. Each of you must approach this in your own way and in your own time and your own heart."

Timothy McGuinn, the only civilian staff member, asked, "What does the bible say about this? I don't remember reading or hearing anything about it. Father Billy, you are the biblical scholar around here, what does the Big Book say?"

Father Billy Thompson answered, "There is nothing there that I am aware of and I've studied the book of Revelation extensively. Maybe someone else here knows something I don't. What about it, James?"

"I am not as well studied as you are Billy, though I know my bible as well as anyone. I agree with you; there is nothing mentioned there that I can find and I've been deep into scripture all week long trying to answer the question. I have been in touch with Rabbi Singer and he confirms the same thing.

We can find nothing in the Old or New Testament to support what is happening. We have come to an agreement about why nothing is in the bible: The bible is a book written for all men, in all nations and we here in the United States, as far as we know, are the only ones that the "dream thing" is touching. We could be wrong, but we don't think so. That is our answer to your question, Timothy."

Father John Phillips, the oldest staff member said, "I think we are at the point in this meeting now where we must move on to the next step. What is the 'pathway' you alluded to at the beginning? Whether we are in complete harmony about the cause of the "dream thing" or does it really matter? There is a particular direction you want us to take and you have been in contact with other clergy of other faiths. The direction must have been agreed upon before you called this meeting. I also heard you say that you haven't checked in with the Vatican yet, are you planning on doing that, or is this a venture without approval? If this venture affects only this country, is the cooperation within our borders something yet to achieve, or is that being addressed now, too? How many church type organizations are involved? Who is running this project? Who is the central figure in charge? There are so many questions racing through my mind right now, I know I'm missing some. James, this is bigger than what we think, isn't it?

"John, you are my dearest friend and closest confidant. It is because of those qualities that I chose you for my Chief of Staff and to be on my advisory board. I thank you for asking the questions and I will try my best to answer them all. Your feedback is essential, as well as from all of you here in this meeting today.

The pathway is complicated and yet simple, but has not been approved by His Holiness yet. Yes, I will contact the Vatican before we actually start walking the path. All the other faith communities are planning to walk with us, but I am the central figure for making the arrangements and planning the events in this area of the country. There are other central figures in other parts of America.

We are separating the internal boarders into nine different segments: northwest, southwest, northwest central, southwest central and so on until the east coast which will be divided in three segments. You asked about how many people are involved. The number of mosques, temple and churches, that I know about now, are over three thousand in my segment, so I assume there are similar numbers in the other eight segments. There probably are a whole lot more in the northeast. You do the math. There are a staggering number of people who have been affected by this thing and are involved one way or another. I believe there will be more as time goes on. We are so organized in such a short period of time that it is mind boggling. This is such a short time line and yet, so much has been accomplished, it's just another reason I know we are on the right track."

Fran, the civilian, asked' "All right James what is the right track? What is it you will be asking Rome? What is it you want of us?"

The Cardinal answered, "All right here it is: Penance, Prayer and Pressure. So simple. So complicated. I will be asking, as will other Cardinals in the U.S., the Holy Father to allow us to take on the government of this country. Our efforts, our pathway will be to change the direction our nation has taken and redirect it to what our founding fathers truly intended. We have to get God back. This cannot be done without the complete cooperation with the majority of American Citizens. This can only happen through penance and prayer. It is my belief that the process has already started for those of us who have been affected. Our prayer life has changed. All our prayers, our communication with God, have become pleading for forgiveness. It is such a basic part of the hearts of the faithful to pray, and our efforts to pray end up with us requesting forgiveness each time. Our pathway has been chosen for us and we must walk that way or be lost forever.

John, my dear friend, you asked if it is bigger that we think. I believe it is bigger than any of us could imagine. I think we have been given a task and if we don't accept that task, if we don't correct the wrong, if we do nothing,

I believe we are looking at the end of the United States as we know it.

Our prayers of requested forgiveness must now become intentional. We cannot start off in one direction and have our prayer turn to something else. We must all pray for forgiveness, but know the reason for the petition. We have either done nothing or not done enough to stop them from removing Our God from our government. This is our prayer for forgiveness but we must all pray it together.

It must be a week of coming together; a week of unity and solidarity, enclosed in prayer. One whole week, six days of constant prayers, that end with the Sabbath. The last day will change the nation and it will be realized on that day. It has to be public; it cannot be hidden away in our places of worship or our homes.

The government and the world must become aware of our togetherness and our determination to set things right, to correct that which has been wrongly put in place in our nation. It must be known that 'we the people' are the voice of America. This voice must be loud enough to make an everlasting impression on the congress, the house, the senate, and the president, because we have to change their minds and open their hearts to Our Lord and Our God. We have to change the course that this nation has taken, change it forever.

The pressure I speak of is the outcome of the method we must pursue with public prayer and solidarity. I have no idea if any of the senators or representatives has been affected by this "dream thing", but it doesn't matter. So many of the faithful have been affected and the numbers will speak loudly to this generation of congress and the generations to come. The prayers will keep us together and the pressure will be placed on congress to bring us back to God. If we change our nation's direction we can change the direction God is facing. If we right our path, He will hear our pleading; He will turn to face His people again. This is the pathway of which I will speak to the Vatican."

Father John Phillips responded, "Wow! I guess you have answered all my questions and I also think you have convinced me that this is a venture that must be taken. I can find no fault in the direction or fault the reason for the walk. I have not been affected and I don't think I want the experience, from what you say, and I don't feel slighted about not being included either. I have known you a long time James and I think the world of you for a number of reasons, not the least is my respect for your insights. Over the years I've learned that when you are on a roll and are sure of yourself, to get out of your way.

I have decided that the pathway you have chosen is correct and your intent is pure so I will do all in my power to assist you in this endeavor. I suggest the same from all who are present in this room."

James Cardinal Roan sat back in the chair and for the first time realized that he was sweating profusely. The effort he put forth for the explanation had been very taxing on him and he wasn't a young man anymore. His full head of white hair topped with the red skullcap was impressive. The red sash around his waist accented the black uniform of all priests. James was in his mid-seventies but looked like a much younger person, mostly because of his slender, tall frame. He worked out daily in the exercise room which his predecessor had installed on the second floor. He was an impressive man. The house they were in was a renaissance style home, but James kept his private quarters simple.

He didn't like the elaborate surroundings he had to work in, so his private rooms contained little accents, other than a large quantity of books on almost any subject, not just religious. James was well read and well respected. He thought he was ready and with God's help, the goals that had been set forth for him and the others would be achieved. He didn't know that the journey he was about to embark upon was going to stretch him to his breaking point.

CHAPTER TWELVE

FATHER TOM'S VISIT

Father Tom Kennedy, in his office at the rectory, was busy on the phone following the directive straight from the Bishop. Tom was calling public facilities large enough to accommodate what they thought might turn out to be a huge crowd of believers coming together for a day or even a week of prayer and penance.

The first and most obvious place he contacted was the ball field. The stadium would definitely be large enough, maybe too large. Tom was closer to the people in his parish than the Bishop and didn't have the same expectations of a large crowd that his Eminence had, but Tom followed his wishes and made the calls anyway. The Business Manager, Bobby Tulane, was not receptive to the idea, not so much that it involved a group of "Religious Fanatics", a term he kept to himself during the conversation with the priest, but because there was no mention of payment. Bobby, if nothing else, was frugal, not so much at home as he was with his monetary responsibilities at work. So with Bobby, "no money no deal", was his rule. He was open to religious organizations. He had graciously approved the Billy Graham Revival Meeting that filled the stadium, last year. The big difference was that money was mentioned right away in the first part of the conversation with Billy's people. Tom had not been given the authority to rent any facility and he now wondered how his quest would be accomplished.

There was a college on the north side of town that had a pretty good sized stadium, but it was not one of the many religious colleges that could have given him an "edge' to use to getting the commitment he was looking for. He called anyway. He was connected to Andrew Wright, the Manager of Operations for the college. Tom started the spiel he had memorized, by that time, but was interrupted by Andrew half way through his speech. "I want you to use us. I need for you to know how important it is to me that you use our field. It happened months ago. I had a dream that our stadium filled with people praying, a lot of people. I didn't know what it meant until now. The dream kept coming back to me almost every night. It almost drove me crazy. I would wake up from the dream and felt like I needed to do something. I didn't know what I needed to do until you called. I'm not a Catholic, Father, but I feel like you are the reason I have been having these dreams. I would never have thought that before, but now I'm convinced: you are the reason!" Tom was left with no words, so finally he thanked Andrew and hung up the phone.

For a while he sat and absorbed what had just happened. He was no longer surprised by the unexpected events that suddenly jumped into his life, since the day the confession of the small boy started the chain. As each event unfolded, his ability to deal with the abnormal became less of a burden. Nothing in his past helped him deal with these happenings, but each one helped him deal with the next that appeared.

He reflected on the beginning, the terrible gut feeling he had listening to the kid in the confessional, the amazement he experienced hearing about the disturbing dreams others spoke of, that he, too, was having. He thought how different it was, that not only were the parishioners complaining but the religious in the community, too. He recalled the stories he heard, that sounded like bad science fiction movies, they told to each other when gathered in the church basement. A reason, a direction and a plan all came from that meeting, which in itself was unbelievable, considering all the circumstances that brought the diverse group together. Yet here he was, trying and now accomplishing the task of locating a place to have their "Day of Prayer" that could very easily turn into a "Week of Prayer", if the Cardinal had his way and the people agreed.

He was sitting back in his office, in an overstuffed chair; slouching a little, letting himself drift off into a kind of dream state, though not asleep. His mind was going over all things related to the abnormalities known to him. He was almost meditating on the happenings but this meditation was different. This dream state of awareness was different. It was almost a fog or mist that surrounded him, yet it did not alarm him, it comforted him. He relaxed even more. This was not the experience of falling asleep which all people, at one time or another, have just before slumber. Tom was very much aware of all that was going on around him and the thoughts that filled his head.

Through the fog, Tom made out two figures in his office. One of the two men was leaning against the corner of the console table in front of the window; the other was standing with his arms crossed, to the right of the table. There was nothing unusual about their appearance other than they showed up unexpectedly. Their sudden presence had no effect on Tom's state of mind. He was not alarmed, curious, distraught, apprehensive, or concerned about his visitors. He was very receptive to their arrival.

For some unknown reason he knew that one of them was going to speak first, so he sat just looking at his visitors until the taller of the two spoke. "Tom, you are a good man, a good priest and a true follower of Jesus." There followed a great silence while the words sunk into Tom's conscious mind. Why was the man telling him that? The other man spoke, "Do you know what you are doing or even more important why?" It was Tom's turn to talk, "I'm not sure what you are asking. What am I doing about what?" The man leaning against the table spoke, "You are calling around the city trying to find a place to gather for prayer. Do you know why?" Tom, still in the semi-dream state, responded, "How did you know I was calling? And yes I know why!"

Again the taller man spoke, "There is a lot we know and you will soon know as well. You may think you know why you are making these phone calls, but there is so much more than you realize. Tom, we are here to help you understand how important it is what you and the other believers are doing. The "why" is what we need to talk about." "Okay, we'll talk about 'Why'. Why do you know my name and I don't know yours?" asked the priest.

The man leaning against the table stood erect and told Tom, "You are right, we should have introduced ourselves. It was rude of us. I'm Jude, son of James also called Thaddeus, and this is Augustine of Hippo, also known as Austin. We have come to you and for all the believers throughout the world so you can better understand what you have undertaken is the most important venture any human has ever attempted and it is essential you do the very best you can. The world, as you know it, depends on you." Tom was dumbfounded! Especially in his dream-like state, he found it hard to comprehend what he had just heard. "St. Jude and St. Augustine right here in my office? Right here in front of me? Are you serious?" Augustine answered, "Serious is a good word. It best describes why we are here. This is a very serious situation and the consequences of your actions are very serious. The believers have recognized that you all have forced God to turn His face away from you. Now you are going to try to get His attention through prayer and penance. You must all understand that your efforts have to succeed. The believers must be of pure heart and true of feelings. We know there will be some who will enter into this endeavor half heartily. That number must not reach even 10% of the believers. Tom, it has to be an all-out effort."

Tom sat numb in his chair, still not totally awake, yet not asleep, but his mind was fully awake and he was beginning to grasp the intensity his visitors were trying to instill within him. "How can I make them understand when I don't fully understand myself? I know you are on a special mission to assist us with this thing, but I don't think II have the full picture. Do I?"

Jude answered, "Not one of you understands. Not one of you. If you don't achieve your goal, it's the end of the world for you. You have only one of the Trinity who will listen now. The Spirit has done all that can be done to help you all understand the reasons, the situation and how grave it is. You didn't totally understand. The Father can only be influenced now by the one who was human, too. You, as the human race, must turn Jesus' face towards you. Tom, it's your last chance. God loves you and it is because of this love that He has listened to what you have all asked of Him. You just didn't understand what you were asking. You didn't understand at all. You should have understood how much your actions would affect the world to come. You didn't! God is so very sad right now. We are here to help you understand that."

Tom responded, "I know what we've done. I even know when some of it happened. I remember when it first started with the legalization of abortion and how it continued with removing God from our schools and then our government. I am ashamed of what we did. I'm ashamed of what we didn't do. Now we have a direction and I think it is a sound decision. What can I do to make it better?"

Augustine spoke, "The effort must first be real and then combined. All peoples and government must come together for the one purpose. All religions must become one in this time of prayer and penance. The government must be involved by changing the direction America is going and put God back in the place where He belongs and was so many years ago. The heart of the people, the people of government, the people of religion, the people of prayer and penance must be true and faithful. Tom, it will be easier to be pure of heart in prayer than in penance but the believers must have a true act of contrition in their hearts and minds. You must take this message to them. We are here to help you do that."

"St. Augustine, I am but one man, I'm neither a Bishop nor a Cardinal. How do you expect me to do these things?

Jude answered Tom, "You are one man but there are three of us now. I myself, take on the impossible all the time and look at the life of my friend, does he not prove to you that prayer and penance can change a man and even a world. You cannot do these things alone. We could not do this alone. The number three is a strong number and together we three can do what is needed. It was not an accident that we are here today. We chose you because of your heart and your faith, but most of all your ability as an orator. Tom, you are an eloquent speaker and people listen to you when you speak. The faithful come to your mass to hear the sermon and stay to hear next week's."

"Okay how do we get started? If you are here to help, and I certainly pray that you are, what do you want me to do? What do the three of us have to do?" asked Tom.

"You have already started, Tom. You have the field and you have believers coming to the day of prayer. We will go to the Cardinal and convince him to let you be the keynote speaker. You have to prepare your speech. You can start there. Keep in mind this will be the most important talk you have ever given. You must also arrange for the media to cover the event. The newspaper, television and radio must be represented that day and they must hear you. You must arrange that as well." Augustine told him.

Without a verbal response to his visitors, Tom fell into a deep sleep and the two saints let him rest alone.

The experience had been very emotional and stressful, though Tom didn't know it. Two hours passed and when he awoke the office was absent the visitors and the foggy mist. Unlike a dream, Tom had total recall of what had happened. He understood his mission and accepted its gravity as well as the assistance promised.

Tom also accepted that he had been visited by two saints whom he had greatly admired throughout his whole life. St Augustine, the playboy saint, was the patron of the grade school he attended which bore his name. The nuns used every opportunity to tell their stories concerning the saint.

"Augustine was lost, his soul destined for the fires of hell because of his worldly ways, but his mother was relentless in her prayer life. She went to Mass daily and knelt in prayer for the conversion of her wayward son. God listened to her years of prayer and turned Augustine's life around. He became the bishop of Hippo and one of our church's greatest saints." This was the story all the Catholic children at St. Augustine Grade School heard from the nuns and there was a sprinkling of truth in the story. It was the nun's story that brought his attention to the saint, but it was the real story of his life that made Augustine special to Tom.

Tom shared his admiration of Jude with thousands of other faithful because of Danny & Marlo Thomas and their work with the hospital that bore St Jude's name and worked real miracles on the sick children admitted there. St Jude, the patron saint of the impossible, was chosen with great care to represent the hospital. It was the correct choice.

Now that he was fully awake and aware of his need to succeed, he picked up the phone, not to call another director of operations to find an appropriate place for the gathering, but the bishop. The second ring was interrupted by the bishop answering. "Hello." "This is Fr. Tom Kennedy; I was calling to let you know...." "Tom, I need to talk to you. I'm so glad you called. I was just about to pick up the phone to call you. I want you to be the keynote speaker at the event."

CHAPTER THIRTEEN

THE DAY OF PRAYER

It was a pleasant day with temperatures in the higher 60's. A clear sky dotted with feather clouds enhanced the comfortable early summer day. Father Thomas Kennedy stood on the platform, erected for the day of prayer, in the middle of the football field belonging to the small college. The cardinal made some announcements about the facility, thanked the college and their attendees, said a short prayer, and introduced the priest to the crowd that had gathered there. When Tom walked to the five clumped microphones on the stand, he noticed for the first time all the television cameras situated in the middle of the center aisle, not more than twenty feet away from the platform. He was not unhappy to see them there. He looked for other reporters in the crowd. They were all there sitting with the believers. Some were from the newspapers, some the radio and others he recognized as television reporters. He counted about twenty in attendance. And so he began.

"There lived a long time ago in a small village at the foothills of the great mountain range in Colorado, a man in his late 50's, married to a woman in her early 40's. For nine years they had been married, they tried to start their family, with no success. On her 49th birthday she got the news, when she visited the family doctor, that she was pregnant. When she got back home and shared the news with her husband they knelt together in prayer, to thank the Lord for the gift of a child. They were overjoyed and counted not the months, not the weeks but the days until they would be a family of three. Each night before going to bed, they would kneel together in the bedroom of their small cottage and thank God. The husband would secretly pray for a boy and the wife would pray alone for a girl, but most importantly they prayed for a healthy child.

In the middle of July they became three. A baby boy was given to the couple; a healthy, beautiful boy that brought tears of gratitude to the eyes of the man. Deep in his heart the man had doubted he would ever be a father without adopting some other person's baby. His elderly mother had made that suggestion before his wife found out she was pregnant. His joy, therefore, was overwhelming, as he looked down into the crib and accepted the miracle in front of him.

The boy grew strong and made a place for himself in the village with the other children at play. The village was small enough that the adults knew all children by name. He was known and loved by all.

In his seventeenth year the boy started to become argumentative with both his parents, but mostly with his father. What pursued were not debates, but fights. The man, now in his declining years, was not strong enough to endure the exhaustion of the emotional encounters. He tried to debate but failed and his answers were never enough to satisfy his son, no matter what the topic. The son and the father could barely have a civil moment together. The man's wife was in tears more than not. The family meals that used to be a time of celebrating, now became a time of bitter silence.

The boy had always been a terrific athlete, excelling at any competitive sport, but basketball was where he truly shined. The man was not responsible for the boy's excellent sport ability. The man could not teach the boy any sports; he was too old, so the boy had to learn on his own. He was tall enough to play the center position. His keen eye and able hands proved to be a combination capable of hoop shots others wouldn't try. He was constantly the top scorer in the league of the surrounding schools. It was at a basketball game in the winter of the boy's senior year that it happened. The final nail was driven into the old man's heart.

The team was struggling in the second half with the score only a couple of points apart at any time. The lead was exchanged over and over. The boy's school started yelling his name in anticipation of him getting the ball and making the difficult shots to win the game. The old man was sitting on the bottom seat of the bleachers. The intensity of the game affected everyone, including the father. Standing up from his seated position, he joined the school crowd, yelling for his son to win the game. He wanted so much to be a part of the scene in front of him that he lost the reality of where he was standing. Soon he found himself on the court moving to the right and then the left as the ball was dribbled and passed from one side to the other. With only two seconds left and the winning score resting on the home team's ability to make two baskets to win and one to tie, the old man inched his way onto the playing floor. The boy pushed the ball into the air from behind the free shot line and watched as it made its way to the hoop. At the same time, a shrill whistle broke the deadly silence, as all eyes in the gymnasium focused on the ball in flight and every breath was being held. The ball swooshed through the hoop to tie the game at 58 to 58, with no time left on the clock, but there was that whistle from one of the referees.

Interference, on the old man's part, was the call against the team and it negated the tying hoop. The other team was allowed two free shots due to the foul, both of which were made, ending the game with a loss for his son's team. The boy stood in the middle of the court glaring at his father, his face getting redder with anger as the seconds ticked away. The crowd became aware of the boy and a heavy silence again filled the room. The old man looked into his son's eyes and saw a hatred he had not seen before.

'I hate you.' He screamed at the top of his voice. 'I hate you so much I never want to see you again. You have destroyed my life. I can't stand the sight of you. I want you to die. Leave me alone!' cried the boy. The old man turned around, tears streaming down his face and walked out of the school's gymnasium. Into the dark night and new fallen snow, the old man walked away from his son. He was never seen again. His foot prints in the snow just disappeared. There was no trace of the old man ever found."

Tom stopped talking for a short while, allowing the story to soak in before addressing his audience again. "The old man listened to his son. He did what the boy wanted, even though it hurt the old man to do so. He loved his son, but he left him. We have gathered here today because Our Father has listened to us, His children, and responded with the same love that the old man had.

For over a decade we have asked God to go away. I don't have to name the times and the places where this has been accomplished. We are all very much aware of what we, in the United States, have done to turn God away. He has listened and has turned away from us. We can't allow this situation to continue. My friends in Christ, if we do, it will mean the end of the world. I'm not exaggerating. I mean exactly what I said. As God is my witness, the end of the world will result if we do not turn God's face back toward us. Most of us here today have had some evidence to prove what I say. It may be the main reason you are in attendance. You know in your heart that I am speaking the truth."

Tom again paused. He could not see them, but he was absolutely positive that his two previous visitors were with him on the stage. Their support had become very important to Tom and he was happy they were present. "The church has called for prayer and penance from its faithful. I know there are many of you here today who are of a different faith. Let us all unite, in this endeavor, into one faith in our one God. One faith in God with the power of prayer behind us, united we must stand. One faith in God with the power of true penance within us, we must stand. With one purpose only and that is to save our world from its imminent destruction. We must stand together and united, we must beg God to turn His face back to us. These acts must be pure of intent, pure of mind and heart. We must call from the depths of our faith to Our God. What we start here today, what we have already started, is the most important act mankind has taken on, by itself, from the beginning of creation. Two thousand years ago God became man and it is only through His intersession and His help that we still have this world today. As we pray for forgiveness, as we pray for our salvation, as we pray to God, begging Him to turn around, we must pray with our whole heart, our whole mind and our whole soul. We will be joined by the believers, the faithful, through thought and heart, dedicated to the same purpose, throughout the whole country. The United States is wholly involved in this holy crusade simultaneously. It has to be that way. The prayers must be united and loud."

Tom stepped away from the microphone and James Cardinal Roan approached the front of the stage. "Over the years my prayer life has been very simple. At times I only say the holy name of Jesus over and over. It gives me great comfort to know He listens to just the mention of His name. Of course the mass is the ultimate prayer and also provides me with great comfort. However, there are more than just Catholics in attendance. This faith community, who gathers today, comes here from different faiths other than my Christian brethren. I recognize our Jewish believers who have come for the same purpose. With all due respect to our Jewish brethren, I will respond to the New Testament that commands the Christians to voice our prayers through the name of Our Savior. It teaches that the only way to the Father is through the Son. Therefore I ask all the believers to come together in one voice as we start our prayer. Our Father who art in heaven..........."

CHAPTER FOURTEEN

THE BEGINNING

In the olden times, God spoke to His people all the time. The Old Testament tells us that God spoke to His people. In Genesis His conversations with us was constant. Gn. 12: 1 The Lord said to Abram: "Go forth from the land..." and Abram did. He even showed Himself in Gn. 18:1 The Lord appeared to Abraham..." Moses was given the Ten Commandment by God on the mountain, Sinai. Ex. 31:18. They had many conversations back then.

The New Testament does not have that very close relationship with God as evident. The words of God come from His spokesmen, the angels of the Lord. They spoke to St. Joseph, Mary the mother of Jesus and to the shepherds in the fields.

There have been events reported in our history of The Virgin Mary appearing at Lourdes, Fatima and most recently Medjugorje. She came to bring the message of God to His people. The longer we live the farther we have gone away from Our Lord.

Buck was not his real name. His mother was the only one alive now that knew he was named Alvin D' Angelo by his father. He decided at the age of eight that he could stand the name no longer and started calling himself Buck. He couldn't stomach the nicknames: Al, Alvie or A. D. Buck D'Angelo sounded strong to him then and still does today.

The dreams brought him to the meeting in the basement of the church not that long ago. It was as close as he had ever been to a church and he felt totally out of place when he walked in. He didn't consider himself a religious man. He didn't even believe in God when he attended that meeting. As the meeting progressed, he found not all the attendees were religious, God fearing, church goers either. Buck gained a great deal of respect for the people who did have a relationship (or were trying to have a relationship) with God. There was strength in them, not the wimpy personality he assumed they all possessed. "This here biker was changed that night," He would tell anyone who noticed a different man from the one they had previously known. Most of his friends didn't or couldn't, accept the new "biker" and simply walked away from him. There were a few who not only stayed his friends but became closer to Buck and revealed they, too, were believers.

The changes that were most remarkable to Buck himself, were the changes in his prayer life. A life that had not existed before the meeting, it surprised him every time he found himself trying to have a conversation with

God. It was not normal for Buck and yet unconsciously he would start a prayer out of nowhere, with not a thought of the attempt. The prayer was always the same and always without thought or preparation. The prayer rolled through his mind, but was never on his lips.

The prayer was a request for forgiveness and always the same words; "God forgive me for the way I've lived." It was a short prayer, but similar to all the other prayers that had been sent heavenly over the last few weeks.

There were many changes in Buck's life, since the meeting, but one thing that did not change was the reason he went to the meeting. The dreams continued. He would sleep no more than forty-five minutes when he was awakened, breathing hard and reaching out for something he could not grasp. In the dream, which was always the same, he was riding his "hog" at a high speed trying desperately to catch up and overtake something or someone ahead of him on a long, narrow, gravel road. He was never able to see what he was chasing because the dream became so intense it would wake him. The awakening was brutal and sudden; from a deep slumber to alert and disturbed, deeply disturbed.

At a rally, shortly before the meeting, Buck was telling another biker about the "damn dream" and to Buck's surprise the other man was experiencing the same type of dream. They told each other about their failing health brought on by the lack of sleep, the pain of the dreams and the lack of understanding of why it was happening. The other biker, named Big Jim McCrae, told Buck about the meeting and told him that he was going to be there. Buck didn't agree to anything but the meeting never left his mind from that point on. His main hesitation came when Big Jim turned and walked away from him. On the back of Big Jim's colors was stitching surrounding the head of an eagle. It read: "Bikers for Christ".

Now here he was. Attending the Day of Prayer and found he was saying the Lord's Prayer out loud with all the other attendants. He looked around to see if anyone else was out of their element saying the familiar prayer taught by Jesus Himself. There must have been five thousand people sitting in the stands or standing on the field of the sports arena belonging to the college. He looked at the faces, wanting to find someone who was equally out of place as he felt he was. There were some hard hat type workers, some people dressed in jeans and plaid shirts, other guys that looked like they just walked out of the woods, wearing their camouflage jackets, but they all looked like they belonged here.

He shouldn't have gone to the meeting. He shouldn't have come to this prayer meet. He didn't like the changes he was going through. He didn't like losing some of his friends. He didn't like anything that was happening to him. But, he sure as hell didn't like the "damn dreams" either.

The prayers continued. He wanted nothing to do with what was going on and he sure wasn't going to continue praying. He listened to the priest, the same one who was at the meeting; tell a story about a boy and his father. It didn't make any sense to him. The explanation the priest gave for the story sounded like a bunch of bunk to him. He didn't know what he was expecting when he came to the college, but it sure wasn't this.

He didn't know what he was looking for at the meeting in the church basement either and all he got from that was a prayer that kept interrupting his thoughts. The dreams were still there. Buck didn't think this prayer day was going to help with his dreams.

Buck turned from facing in the direction where the priest was standing and started walking towards the exit on the field. He pushed his way through a few of the people who were praying with their eyes shut and their arms reaching to the heavens. Some of the people stepped aside as he made his way through the crowd to the exit. Some were on their knees, heads bent forward and hands folded in front of their chests. Some prayed in silence, some out loud. Many were crying, others seemed to praying in their native tongue (Italian, Spanish, German and French). Buck walked through them all making his way to the exit gate on the opposite end of the field.

He didn't make it there. As his prayer of forgiveness came from nowhere, so did his pleading prayer. Bursting forth from his lips came: "My God, My God, why have you forsaken me?"

The prayer knocked him to his knees and with his arms reaching to the Heavenly Father he again exclaimed: "My God, My God, why have you forsaken me?"

There was a tremendous calm that came over Buck and joy filled his heart. A joy he had never experienced before in this life, a calm he had never known before. Warmth took its place in his very soul. Then Buck heard it: A voice from deep within in him. A voice that was familiar to him, but not known to him. A voice that was gravely and deep, similar to his own. The voice spoke to Buck one simple truth; "You have turned His face back to you. Rejoice and be glad!" Buck cried out: "He turned! He heard! Praise be the Lord!"

The Evangelist, Jackie Anderson stood before a crowd of twenty thousand in an open field donated by the local Baptist church for this occasion. One of the members of the southern Baptist congregation owned the farm and was more than glad to allow the church to use the back pasture for this purpose.

Jackie was as well known in the south as was Billy Graham throughout America. He had great charisma and taught the word of God with conviction and a pure heart. He was called to preach the Word, but not to become rich from it. After keeping some of the collection for the necessities of his mission he gave the rest to charity.

Jackie preached for about a half hour and called the believers to prayer. As it was done all over the United Stated on this day, all the Christian communities started with the Lord's Prayer. The prayers were sent up with more passion and commitment than usual. Tears flowed down the cheeks of the ones praying. Arms were lifted to the sky and the words of petition poured from the mouths of the faithful.

Three sisters, Mary, Fran and Elizabeth lived in the farm house left by their father when he died, over thirty years ago. They never moved from the homestead, never married, nor missed a Sunday or Wednesday at church. They did not till the one hundred acres their father had worked all his life. Their life was not in the dirt of the fields, but in the work they performed at the Baptist church.

Their devotion to the sick, the needy, the poor, the shut-ins and the hungry was continuous. They had little money, but a lot of time. And their time was spent on others. They were well known and well-loved in the southern community of Sweet River, GA.

The three sisters were sitting two rows back from the stage and, if the aisle hadn't been there, almost dead center. They had not experienced the dreams but each one of the sisters felt something wrong while ministering to their flock. The gratitude was not there anymore. It was one of the few gifts that the sisters allowed themselves and enjoyed receiving. It started a couple of weeks ago when Old Mrs. Tremble didn't give them her great smile and want the hugs she always asked for as the sisters gathered themselves ready to leave. Tremble just sat in the overstuffed chair, one of her few belongings, in the old folk's home and said good-by. She wasn't the only one who changed. They would have excused Tremble's actions as just getting old, but it was happening at every stop they made. No "thank you" no "God Bless you" nothing. It was strange at first, but as the weeks went by, it became a major concern and they talked about it a lot.

That is why they were sitting at the revival. Wanting some answers and afraid to ask. They were just praying, these faithful servants. There was no singing. The singing was something they looked forward to and always there was a time for the "Call to the Altar". This was when the sisters could ask the burning question consuming their every moment together. Nothing like what they expected was happening. They sat there waiting for what seemed like hours, but was actually no more than one hour. Finally Fran, the oldest turned to Mary, the youngest and said loud enough for Elizabeth to hear; "Okay we're going." The sister got to their feet and walked in procession up the isle toward the back of the assembly. No one noticed they were on their way out because everyone else was deep in prayer.

In unison, Fran, Mary and Elizabeth in voices loud enough to disturb half the assembly, cried out: "My God, My God why have you abandoned me?" The three sisters cried out three different times which caused the whole congregation of twenty thousand people to stop what they were doing and look to the rear of the assembly. When the third exclamation poured from their inner most beings, the three sisters fell to their knees exhausted.

Mary was holding Fran in an attempt to stop her from dropping to the grass below them. Elizabeth was holding herself up by placing the palms of her hands firmly on the ground, elbows locked. Then almost as if they were picked up by some unseen hands, the three sisters were standing, facing the gatherers.

There was no sign of exhaustion on their faces. It had been replaced by an inner glow that reflected on the face of each of them. At the same time, all three experienced something they had all heard about, at the revivals they had ever attended, but never experienced. They heard the voice of God. Only the voice in their innermost being was not what they had expected God's voice to sound like.

They heard a sweet feminine voice that soothed any fear they might have had. The voice spoke a truth that was not questionable: "You have turned His face back to you. Rejoice and be Glad!" In unison they cried out, "He heard us! He has turned His face back to us. Praise the Lord!"

New York and Florida were hosting the "Day of Prayer" simultaneously by a satellite television connection between the cities' largest synagogues. The crowd was overflowing at both buildings. There were readings from the Torah: portions of Genesis were read by the Rabbi in New York and portions of Exodus were read in Florida. Then they were instructed to start the praying. Both building filled with the sound of English and Hebrew. In both synagogues there were seven men that during the prayers cried out in loud voices: "Eloi, Eloi, lama sabachthani?" "My God, My God why have you forsaken me, far from my prayer, from the words of my cry?" The crowd was brought to silence and turned to see who had cried out so loud to disrupt all the others. The seven men in New York and the seven men in Florida were identified by the congregation and a large circle open up around them. The men went to their knees, crying out, with exhaustion, their quotes from Psalm 22. Then all of their appearances changed. There was something happening to each of the men in sight of all who could see. There was a glow, radiance about them and they looked skywards and appeared to be seeing something, or someone not visible to the others. When all went silent again, the seven men in New York and the seven in Florida stood facing their Jewish brethren to announce one at a time; "The angel of the Lord has come to us and we have been told to spread the good news. Our Lord and Our God had heard our pleas. He has turned His face back to see us again and we are saved. Give glory and praise to Our Lord!" Each one of the fourteen spoke the exact sentence.

Change came very slowly, but it came. The prayer life of the Faithful took on a new and exciting direction. They prayed with a deeper and more real feeling of communication with God. It was now more obvious that He was listening to each word and responding. Tears often accompanied these special times, but now the tears were of great joy, not the weeping they had experienced before. With the prayers came the songs and the songs had deeper, more meaningful words to those who sang.

Some Catholic churches brought out, from the past, a hymn that had been neglected and started using it at all the masses. Soon it caught on and spread throughout all the churches, Catholic and Protestant. *Change Our Hearts* became the Christian National Anthem.

Soon it was adopted by the Jewish Community and with a slight change of words, fit their beliefs as well:

> *Change our hearts this time, Your word says it can be.*
>
> *Change our minds this time, Your life could make us free.*
>
> *We are the people, Your call set apart.*
>
> *Lord, this time, change our hearts."*

One of the most notable changes happened in Alabama. In 2003 District Judge Myron Thompson ordered that the huge monument depicting the Ten Commandments, placed there by Chief Justice Roy Moore, be removed from the state building. There was a massive controversy when Moore refused the order. Eventually the Ten Commandments were taken out of the building. Today the monument stands where it was in 2003.

And so it went throughout the land. Lives were changed and old habits of allowing the unallowable changed as well. The faithful spoke up and the lawgivers listened. The government changed and listened to the will of the faithful. Prayers started public meetings with no rebuke. The Ten Commandments decorated the halls and walls of government buildings. "In God We Trust" again was printed on the face of all our currency. Football, basketball and baseball games started with the teams on their knees, led in prayer by either their coaches or another team member and no one objected.

Timothy Murphy, the catcher for the New Your Yankees, walked out to the pitcher's mound at Yankee Stadium, knelt down on one knee, bowed his head one evening before the second game of a double header. Within two minutes all the members of both the Yankees' and the Dodges' rosters had joined him. The stadium became a quiet as the interior of a deep cave. Everyone in Yankee stadium was joining the conversation with God. Although it didn't last long, it was a huge time and, when Timothy Murphy stood up, a roar came out of the evening crowd that could be heard for miles.

Tom Kennedy's life returned to normal. He still got calls every now and then from people who had found a close relationship with the priest because they shared such a disturbing time in their lives together. The confessional returned to: "Bless me Father for I have sinned. I hit my little brother in the mouth and made him cry." The mass however did not return to what Tom had experienced before the dreams. The mass now seemed to be a glowing declaration of God's love for His children, a love that Tom had never felt before. He looked forward to the next time he could hold up the host and say the words: This is my body... This is my blood... Which shall be shed for you...

The young man, who rebuked his father at the basketball game, eventually followed the old man into the cold, dark, wintery night. The boy couldn't see the old man and the snow had covered his path. He cried out to his father from the very depth of his heart and soul. Tears of loss and fear ran down his face and froze in place. He ran blindly ahead into the storm of a white, blinding sheet of ice and snow. He ran until he could no longer run and sank into the deep snow, exhausted and sorry for what he had done. From nowhere the old man appeared and went to his son's side. The old man was overjoyed and allowed his son to find refuge in his open arms. A place where the boy finally realized was the most desirable place to be and where he belonged. And his father smiled.

ABOUT THE AUTHOR

I have seen our country move closer and closer to reaching the goal of removing all aspects of our Christian-Jewish history from all public parts of our daily lives. These new facts of life bother me, as they bother many of my Christian and Jewish brothers and sisters. My wife, Patt, and I were having a lengthy discussion about the pathway America was traveling when she challenged me. "Why don't you write this down"? No, I was not qualified. Yet, when I sat down at the computer's keyboard, the words flew onto the pages and the thoughts came continuously. I felt like I was doing "the Lord's work" and, boy, was I getting help.

Right in the middle of my work, I was diagnosed with cancer. There were two times over the next three years that I needed to have God listen to the prayers that were being said on my behalf. Both times God's answer was "YES" and both times that answer lengthened my life expectancy.

Those particular, life-giving, answered, prayers re-affirmed my faith and re-affirmed my commitment to the book. I felt, deeply, the book needed publishing. I prayed, hard, that it wasn't my ego, but God's will to which I was responding.

In the little Kansas town of Gardner, south of Kansas City, Patt and I live in an empty nest. We have 6 children, 16 grandchildren and just received a gift of our first "great" grandson. Life is good in Gardner, KS.